Pastiche of Poetry

VOLUME II

N - Z

50 YEARS OF POEMS
ARRANGED ALPHABETICALLY

ROSE KLIX

Address author inquiries and mail orders to:
Custom Writing Services
P.O. Box 5266
Johnson City, TN 37602-5266
Website: http://www.RoseKlix.com
ISBN-13: 978-1481021593
ISBN-10: 1481021591

Library of Congress Control Number: 2012922197
CreateSpace Independent Publishing Platform
North Charleston, South Carolina

Dedications

I gratefully dedicate this two-volume collection of poetry to the special friends who share my interest in writing: my instructors, poetry judges, editors, peers, and writing mentors. They showered me with many discussions of my babblings. A more comprehensive dedications section begins Volume I. Without their assistance and encouragement, this collection would not exist. However, my mentors are not responsible for my final choices of theme, word, line, or form.

Many, many people in several locations influenced the character of my words. The ones I know gather through various writers' organizations in several states. I list them by location in the Acknowledgements section of this Volume II.

Introduction

Pastiche of Poetry represents a potpourri of poems I wrote over a span of fifty years from 1962 through 2012. The poems are arranged alphabetically by title with A-M in Volume I. Those titled N-Z are in this Volume II. The full Introduction is included in Volume I.

A hodgepodge of poems were acknowledged by awards or previous publication. I compiled all of my poetry up to now so that the whole mishmash will live together in one collection.

For anyone curious about the date order when the poems were created, I include a chronological listing, as well as a theme concordance in the back of this Volume II. Please be gentle with my youngest poems. The teenage angst, the love and loss were part of my life and my expressions are those of an immature and less educated rosebud. I chose to leave the poems, basically, as written.

I hope you find at least one enjoyable piece to remind you of your own experiences and enjoyment in this challenging and beautiful world.

Thank you for sharing our poetry time together.

Rose Klix

Natural Home

My nature has become
true to nature. Earth, my
home, displays a fickle
skylight ceiling and
verdant floor sprinkled
with crystals and petals.

I've graduated to
a different rock and
rolling, more fun
to twirl between hard
and soft contrasts,
drink shared energy.

Rocks and trees no longer
bore me, but form foundations,
natural walls and divisions.
I reach goals at mountaintops,
teeter my limitations on cliff edges.
I breathe in life, welcome nature.

*Written in 2009, 2012 White Buffalo Silver Sage Award
and published in* Great Spirit Anthology, Volume II

Natural Love

I love nature.
You are nature.
Naturally it's
natural to love you.

No complications,
no interferences,
no disagreements,
you are my refuge.

My lofty ideas
float infinitely.
You ground me.
It's just your nature.

Naturally it's
natural to love you.
You are nature.
I love nature.

Written in 2010

Negativity

There are nos
      and there are no-nos.
There are noses
      and naïve know-it-alls.

But there are no naughty know-it-alls
      with nervous noses
            who do no-nos for nothing.

Written in 2004, 2007 published in The Open Hearth
and in Tennessee Voices Anthology 2009-10

Neighboring Golf Expectations

a Limerick form

There were two men who planned for sun
whose expectations were par none.
No practicing stroke
seeded nature's joke.
Outdoor timing tricky for fun.

Written in 2009

Neighbor's Fence

a Pirouette form

Yellow and purple iris
divide the straight fence line.
Our side, pretty flowers.
Your dog barks, patrols,
peeks through wooden slats.

Peek through wooden slats,
see manicured lawn,
clipped hedge topiary.
Invited garden guests
sip rum and laugh.

2008 Honorable Mention in PST Annual Mid-South Poetry Festival

Never Insult those Cooks

Never insult those cooks,
who stir from classic books,
yet boil with attitudes.

Chefs burn with passion.
No fair you dashin'
such tasty bad-itudes!

For sweet saucy fashion,
your gratitude
will gain latitude.

Posted online on Poetic Asides *2009*

New Way Vane

Weathervane points to urban sprawl.
North are condominiums.
South is new housing.
East sit brother barns.
West are more people.
What next?
Sidewalks,
curbs, and gutters,
less country,
more urbanity.

2008 published in Barn Charm *chapbook*

New Year Bells

Stop pulling low-pitched
mournful sounds.
Don't toll those church bells
for this new year.

Ring in the New Year.
All tones blend and
chase each other's notes
like children run and laugh.

Don't mark the finish line
of last year nor expect a sad end.
Sing out the notes of a new beginning.
It crests with no sorrowful intentions.

Chime bells; herald peace,
love, hope. Keep them alive.
Louder now. I must not hear
grief for the new year.

Don't be afraid. Calendars change.
New cycles challenge me
to renew my aspirations,
my dreams, my objectives.

Peal the bells joyfully.
Welcome a new chance
to terminate the past and
start again with harmony.

Written in 2011

Nine-Year Itch

Dedicated to my fifth-grade teacher

I took
nine years
to fully
discover writing.

Nine years before
Mrs. Speakman
taught me.

She started my
lifetime
longing
for publication.

Those first
nine years
were easiest.

Written in 2010

No One Better

There,
aren't you charmed
by his smile?
That flirty grin
unarmed me
with purple lies.
No one better
suited my insecurities.

Written in 1979

No Place

His son's dog whimpered.
The man's hold on the leash tightened.
He stopped the park's water fountain,
wiped the water beads from his chin, and
hand-combed his thin white strands.

He settled on a shaded bench
where the beautiful golden
Spitz-cross sighed into place.
Her curled tail wagged at friendly glances.
What to do with the dog?

The overcrowded city pound
accepted no more. The newspaper,
recorded his unmarried son's obituary,
also reported dozens of pet giveaways.
Retirement home denied pet ownership.

A deep sigh bent the man's toes
where the dog's head rested.
Golden brown eyes fluttered
and looked up at the man.
He resisted a pat on her head.

No home for a dog left behind.
Pounds and cemeteries fill too soon.
No available plot for a careless driver
who lost his race with death.
No place to reconcile.

A lovely jogger smiles and stops to pet the dog.

*2010 2nd and 3rd Places (two judges) in
PST Annual Mid-South Poetry Festival*

November Fall

a Concrete or Picture form

I'll
hold on
to the very last
ounce of sap until
everyone else are in
places I can only imagine,
where leaves never fall,
no strong winds blow
away my faith. This time,
I'll not prematurely release
precious ones. November
leaves hold on until
their forever.
I will,
too.

2005 published in Schrom Hills Park *chapbook,*
and 2010 Spiritual Reflections *anthology by PST-NE,*
and 2012 in Common Ground Herald

Now

"Now" is so definite
yet meaningless.
"Now" is never gone.

An instant later
another "now" appears.
The old one disappears.

"Now" never really goes.
Its meaning is perpetuated.
"Now" is so infinite.

Posted online on Poetic Asides *2009*

Obedience Trained

from that first day
      he fought against the leash
he sat, he spoke, but didn't heel

commands were few
      obedience was sparse
one day he wandered off

without his tags
      he was free to be
to belong to no one

his favorite dish offered
      I called and called
he didn't come

      the trail home
      became cold
he was hungry

freedom came with a price
      he was challenged on every block
his marks would not remain

his new mistress found him cold and lonely
      she blamed me for his neglect
then he sat, he spoke, but didn't heel

he lapped up her offerings
      ignored her commands
his leash was too tight
      he was off again

Written in 2004,
2005 published in Iguana Review *Summer edition*

Ode to a Pomegranate

We know little of you, oh, ancient fruit of
goddess legend. Oh, tasty thought.
Your odd shape, like a submarine mine,
round, rough, unappealing, explodes with flavor.

While we ponder your healthful characteristics,
wars are waged and starving millions complain.
Yet you are the cure all, to be all. Your seeds
squeezed of their nectar, sucked up as a health potion.

My first whispered love, awakened awareness,
showed me your inner safe. We enjoyed
each seed, one by one, until I traveled
to Hades with Persephone.

Now your life juice is sucked from a bottle
to be part of a gang of the cool group.
You haven't really changed. Neither has war or love.
I just pity the unfortunate and kiss a different face.

Written in 2004,
2009 Honorable Mention at National Federation
of State Poetry Societies (NFSPS)

Ode to a Telephone

E-mail is an instant
lob into your court,
even when you're
supposedly not available.

Even your answering
machine gives me
a sense of connection
inside your world.

Still I'd rather hear
your human voice.
Please don't use
the mechanical one.

LOL is not nearly
as infectious as
your giggle in my ear
through my receiver.

2009 posted on Poetic Asides

Old Movies

Never die -- They just

Fade into late night

TV

1977 Written for Creative Writing class at DWU
and published in 1978 Prairie Winds *Volume XXVIII*

Old Glory

Faded now,
edges frayed.
Proudly dance
in the wind,
wave your colors
at passing trains.
Folds snappy,
colors pure.
Symbolism fresh,
not new.

Face north,
wave south –
no sides taken,
represent all.
Furl with the wind,
stand firm.
Red, white and blue
represents brown,
black, red, white,
and yellow.

We all salute you.

Written in 2002 on one year anniversary of 9/11

On On On

A cobblestone sidewalk
displayed a chalked arrow
and scribbled words:
   ON ON ON

I turned, looked again
at drawn arrow feathers.
Upside down it said,
   NO NO NO

Farther down, ON ON ON
marked my path again.
At the green light I was
encouraged to go ON OVER.

I crossed the street.
No messages on either corner.
None halfway up the main block.
I walked the side street.

A similar scuffed chalked arrow
walked me past a construction site.
Another scribbled one
pointed to a pub.

Clever advertisement?
A friend's written directions?
A stray path? Temptation?
I peeked in, but didn't enter.

2005 published in Faith and Spirit *chapbook*

Open the Rosebud

meditate free
write from the heart

fully experience
soul's life purpose

unrestricted love
pollinates ideas

no deposit no return
on my memories

mind float
open the rosebud

Written in 2008

Opponents

When we met we knew we were different,
        but we complemented each other,
                didn't we?

I am soft-spoken.
        You were stern.
I observe people.
        You involved yourself with them.
I impatiently want improvements.
        You steadily made revisions.
I like animals.
        You adored them.
I observe the outdoors.
        You were absorbed into nature.
I understand that people have limitations.
        You expected so much of yourself and others.

I loved you.
        You loved me,
                but . . .
        we are too different,
                aren't we?

Written in 1985

Our Cages

Stop it! Don't cage me.
I'm seventeen. Set me free.
Let me just be me.
Don't protect me.
Don't restrict me.
Leave me alone.

* * *

Mom's feeble and alone.
Don't cage her.
I'll protect her, help her.
I must restrain her.
She pushed me away.
Soon, she will truly be free.

Written in 2009

Our Division

a Beech form

Golf course
keeps your attention,
helps my convention
retention –
my poetry enjoyment source.

Written in 2010

Over Here, Mom

I'm so glad
you are my Brownie leader.
Here I am, Mom.
I wave my hand.
I know the answer.
I volunteer.
I have something to say.
Momma,
am I invisible again?

Written in 1966

Overslept

a Beech form

We're late.
I slept long enough
for your plane take off.
Now you're gruff.
Oh, great!

Written in 2009

Oxygen

Pure clean oxygen,
breathalyzers for purity.
It's against the law
to breathe out toxins.

Written in 2010 (theme = future matters)

Packing a Load

All my bags were stuffed
full of recriminations,
and guilt, without
a sprinkle of self-love.

I dragged that trash
wherever I went,
knotted to each other,
strapped on my waist.

At counseling, you planned
for me to put them away
in the forgiveness garage.
I avoided receipt of joy.

The first weeks, we released
my guilt and anger.
One by one you helped me
untie all their tethers.

Once we un-creased
the pain and mourning,
we folded them
in neatly packed cartons.
The childish feelings belong
stored safely in my mind's attic.
It's all right to remember where
they are and where I have been.

Adult eyes move life forward
without everything brought with me.
I learned to accept
love, forgiveness, and joy.

Written in 1985

Paddle Around

You said,
"Go with the flow."

Instead, I paddled
against the current,
bumped against rocks.
My arms ached.

Once I let go,
I floated effortlessly
downstream.

Written in 2012

*Pahasapa**

an Acrostic form

PAtiently, quietly
      slip through the tranquil sacred grounds,
HAppy hunting grounds
      for centuries of Sioux. Now,
SAnctuary for
      peaceful walks and serene thoughts.
PAtiently, quietly
      slip through the tranquil sacred grounds.

*Pahasapa in Sioux translates as *Black Hills*

Written in 1985

Painful Love

Misdirected
love hurt my
soul, stifled
my existence.

You wanted
me to change,
to be your imagined
female perfection.

I pleased you, but lost
myself. Daughter, sister,
wife, mother, smothered
the parts that are me.

I lost your thoughts,
but found my words.
Alone, I learned
my truer identity.

Written in 1979, posted on Poetic Asides *in 2009*

Palmetto

topped by leaves
like a flapper with a
peacock feathered hat

serious short,
singular trunk
and frivolous leaves

stands proud
through heat
and humidity

palmetto prefers
warm climate,
like me

state seal and flag honors,
license plate pictures
South Carolina adoption

symbolic of
British fleet defeat
at a Palmetto log fort

Written in 2009

Pangram and a Twist

a Pangram form

I vow,
Quary, just no beach
'til min-pin
King Zax is fed!

Published on FanStory.com *in 2008*

Papaw's Possum Recipe

Flumdiddled and penniless,
the Ruritan Society
created a competition carnival.
Busybody neighborhood
davenport gawk-gossipers
encouraged culinary recipes,
formalizing Papaw's
notorious barbequed possum.
Entertainments incorporated
Tennessee's masterpiece
violin fiddler performances,
silhouetted artisans
of tobaccy-stained embroidery
and welcomed preferential
presentations at tourist gatherings
in Appalachian mountaintops.
Plentiful toothpicks, but
no possum leftovers.

2008 awarded 1st *Place in* Poetry for the Intelligentsia *on*
FanStory.com,
3rd *Place at PST Annual Mid-South Poetry Festival and*
2011 in PST-NE anthology Funny you should say that. . .

Paper Promises

a Diamante form

Paper
promises made
aren't easily broken. Right?
Why can't I take you at your word?
Why must I insist on your signature?
I would think that now you would be mature.
I don't want a court fight.
You'll pay for your
caper!

1977 Written for Creative Writing class at DWU

Paper Sack

The paper sack, I was given
to hold my life, sat heavy.

The laughter and good times
floated to the top for us to enjoy.

I didn't expect the bottom to drop out
when I was left with an empty bag.

Written in 2009

Parallel Parking

Aha! A parking space. I approach it slowly,
decide my plan of attack. Rapidly, I turn my wheels
inward to glide against the curb.
Then I back up to the second parking meter.
Luckily there were three spaces open.

I've finished my shopping and return
to where my car patiently awaits my arrival.
I imagine a leer on the van behind me
and discern a giggle from the pick-up in front.
They hemmed in my car both front and back.

I shift into gear and back up inch by inch.
I cannot see the fenders touch, but
fear they are a breath apart. Decimal
by decimal, I pull forward until I'm certain
my hood ornament waved to the car's trailer hitch.

I still cannot clear the front vehicle.
I reverse again. A young man directs me.
I jerk back, accelerate and brake,
but don't trust his hand signals.
He senses my frustration.

"Lady, you've got a good ten inches to go."
After I don't cooperate, he gives up.
I see-saw until the pick-up in front moves
in one fluid motion. I'm no longer
trapped and go home at last.

Written in 1973

Park Planning

Today, I will
rocket to Mars,
slide to my knees,
swing my heels cloud high,
wander through
flowering trees,
read quietly
on a park bench,
run, jump, play ball,
count toadstools,
use my outdoor voice,
and come back again tomorrow.

2005 published in Schrom Hills Park *chapbook*

Park Politics

Radical red chippers
up a tree,
politic to pacifists,
out on a limb,
balance fence sitters.

Chirp Democrats.
Squawk Republicans.
Majority silenced.

Cacophonous filibuster's
primeval chatter.

2005 published in Schrom Hills Park *chapbook*

Passion Fruit

a Glosa form

Dorothy Parker: The Passionate Freudian to His Love

> *So come dwell a while on that distant isle*
> *in the brilliant tropic weather;*
> *where a Freud in need is a Freud indeed,*
> *we'll always be Jung together.*

He was as passionate as passion fruit,
ripe for self-deception wondering who
talked of him and who didn't. His trips
tripped him up with mother figures.
Her engraved invitation stated,
> "So come dwell a while on that distant isle."

Where he rendezvoused, no one knew.
He traveled alone on solo flights to rich solitude
dared not speak of his destination
to contemplate the latest party favors
> "in the brilliant tropic weather."

He was freed within imprisoning walls,
only his lover's ear tuned to hear.
He feared the shadows whispered secrets
in a sanctimonious sanctuary,
> "where a Freud in need is a Freud indeed."

Preparing for the return trip,
he searched the drawers and closets
for love letters he'd squirreled away.
Satisfied they were safe he wrote goodbye as,
> "We'll always be Jung together."

Written in 2012 for Poetic Asides *prompt (a glosa)*

Past Patriotic

I miss patriotic parades
of my youth when
Memorial Day
crowds jockeyed
for lawn chair space.

I've renewed
my repertoire
of loyalty songs
and patriotic hymns.
Fourth of July fireworks

punctuate a military
tattoo ceremony.
Marches of veterans
always carry my tears
in their kettle drums.

Written in 2002

Patience

I.

a Senyru form

Patience looked at its
watch and decided to give
my time back today.

Written in 1988

Patience

II.

an Acrostic form

Patience looked
At its watch and asked
Time to divide
Intervals given
Everyone, every day.
Nice of the old man to
Choose an hour for me.
Even though I lost patience.

Written in 2008

Patient Love

Love is quiet patience
with small seeds of wisdom,
fertilizer for care-nourished
sprouts to blossom.
Time owns patience.

God waits through our decades,
watches and nudges tender
growths – quietly applauds
each step closer to Him
on His patient elastic thread.

Before I ask for change,
I demand it already be done.
Hope and grace expectations
are too long a stretch
for my impatient spirit.

Please, God, renew my patience
to wait for change. Refresh
others who wait for my
metamorphosis.

I accept Your love
and impatiently await your
promised kingdom.

1998 published in The Messenger
and 2005 in Faith and Spirit *chapbook*

Patriot

an Acrostic form

Prayers to our maker,
Allegiance to the nation,
Trust in God,
Religious freedom,
Independent and free.
Others envy
Treasures we have.

Written in 2002

Pay Off

The highest high
is when you ask,
"What's the loan
pay off amount?"
Then actually write
that amount.
on the check.

Written in 1990

Peace Chief

Attakullakulla, Little Carpenter
Cherokee Peace Chief from 1758-1780

Long Hair Clan,
produced peace chiefs.
He wore yellow,
with his black hair,
elaborately braided,
head up,
walked proud.

"...the most important
Indian of his day,"
powerful diplomat, politician,
united his Cherokee people,
brokered land treaty
talked of past times,

remembered unlimited fields,
green grass, much deer,
warm fires, quiet nights.
He frowned at talk
of vengeful attacks.
His voice was silenced.

Whites invaded hunting lands and homes.
Peace government ended.
Son, Dragging Canoe,
assisted war parties.
Both men died before Trail of Tears
relocated lives and split their
Eastern Band and Cherokee Nation.
Descendants maintain peaceful legacy.

Written in 2009

Peaks and Valleys

a Lyric form

Mountain peaks too high
valleys low below.
Cliffs pierce azure sky.
Winds forever blow.

My confused soul stays
cluttered with gray thoughts,
takes control of days.
I've tied messy knots.

Goals: unreachable,
accomplishments few,
my life's not tenable.
Next stop: to view You.

Written in 2009

Pear Shape

a Haiku form

Pear shape
longs for elusive banana shape
turns apple shaped.

Written in 2005

Personal Attention

For three months, I mourned.

Your doctor's office called
to confirm your next appointment.

"I am so, so sorry she died.
       No one marked her chart."

I suggested she file
your inactive records.

What will they charge
for such personal attention?

Written in 2009

Pest Planning

Ant Hill City takes the prize
for most natural housing,
available dirt cheap.

Renewable resources,
organically piped directly
from the Creator.

View unimaginable features,
in ecologically friendly designs.
Come to their Open Pit Day.

Written in 2009

Picayune Pests

No open invitation
welcome mat
this winter,
nor any time.
No burnt toast
crumbs served here.

A million times
bigger than
your ant army,
I'll smack you,
drown you dead,
squash you to trash.

Unwelcome guests
trail mark
kitchen counters,
smart from my
heavy-handed
hostess repartee.

Don't bother me
nor someone else.
Exit. Crawl
through a hole.
Take the darn
silverfish
with you too.

Written in 2004

Pieced Together

I remember we were interlocked
pieces of the same jigsaw puzzle.
Now our picture sits incomplete.

Leave, if you can't compete with verse
and line, rhymed or not. The writing is mine.
Pens create beautiful verse while spirits die.

Life will not stay simple and fair
but becomes esoterical intimidation.
I go back in time to listen for silence.

Eyes close, cleanse mind, head bobs
with the rhythm of the rain on fence posts.
Clear, fresh, crisp air I breathe deeply.

I meditate on roots, leaves, weeds,
and thorns. The sages tell me,
"You're nothing until you bloom."

Time for my poems to speak.
I'll write, write and write my inkwell dry
until I depart, return, and piece together again.

Written in 2008

Places I Once Lived

Under the shadow of Dinosaur Hill
thirty miles from Mount Rushmore,
I learned of olden times from my ancestors
and political leaders who greet the tourists.

On the windy plains in Mitchell's Corn Palace
I earned my bachelor's degree. I practiced
teaching at Plankinton's Reform School,
where I learned positive peer culture.

Bison sat close to the North Dakota border.
With a silo for a skyscraper, it was central
to ranch lands and wheat fields. My high school
students taught me one very long year.

Recreation was limited to a six-lane bowling alley,
seven-and-a-half days of team play per week.
The Main Street drag included one bar,
a grocery store, and three churches.

In Helena, Montana a sleeping giant
overlooked us from the hill.
Across the street lived a clown,
who shot pop bottle rockets at balloons.

At the Iraklion Air Station, Crete, Greece
I worked as the JAG's paralegal.
I learned to appreciate America, running water,
telephone clarity, and reliable electricity.

In Greenbelt, Maryland, I escaped the beltway,
claimed I was allergic to highways ending in 95.
Then I retired to write and moved to Tennessee.

Written in 2012 in Jesse Graves Workshop, sponsored by PST-NE

Please Understand

Please
>like me,
>trust me,
>understand me,

And
>need me,
>want me,
>take me,

But
>most of
>all
>love me.

Don't
>laugh at me,
>ignore me,
>be jealous,

Or
>share me,
>leave me,
>forget me,

And
>be true.
>Just
>love me.

Written in 1971

Please - Why?

Please - why should I say that?
Thank you - what does that mean?
Polite - why should I be?

Love - is there such a thing?
In this world of hurry up, don't bother me,
how can there be such a thing?

Shh. Secrets. Find the answers.

1977 Written in DWU Creative Writing class

Poe Toaster Speaks Out

- on the bicentennial of Edgar Allan Poe's birth January 19, 1809

Poe remains where Poe died.
His life wrestled with death whether
mad genius or tormented artist.
I again toast his birth at graveside,
my face veiled in mourning obscurity.

His soul visits many abodes where
he survived Boston, edited Richmond,
published and critiqued Philadelphia.
Baltimore Ravens honor his poem. But
many thought *nevermore* were they a singular force.

Father of mystery, perpetual Gothic,
forward thinker and elegist, penned
macabre morbid tragedy, love, and loss.
Gambling with alcohol and poisoned
politics, he congested his dying brain.

I leave one rose for Poe, one for wife Virginia
one more for his mother-in-law Maria Clemm.
I toast him with traditional French Cognac.
His life was forty tortured years. Now I celebrate
two centuries of his birth, his life, and evermore.

> ** The Poe Toaster is a mysterious black clad figure*
> *who leaves three roses and a bottle of French Cognac*
> *on Edgar Allan Poe's Baltimore, Maryland gravesite*
> *on the anniversary of his birth.*

Written in 2009

Poet of Life

I started with clean pages.
You handed me free will.
I thought my poem was my own.

All life has but one real Poet,
who penned the natural laws
with consequences and rewards.

I'm not the only author of my life.
He edits, critiques, and fact-checks
to ensure I'll reach His great publishing house.

Posted on Poetic Asides *in 2009*

Poetic License

He has
written a glossary
on poetic license
which no longer exists.
Is that right?

1977 Written for Creative Writing class at DWU

Poetry

an Acrostic form

Polished words,
Open-hearted,
Exaggerated details,
Trite – sometimes,
Romance at its sentimentalist,
Young lover's voice.

1977 Written for Creative Writing class at DWU

Pom Crazy

I.

I want a Pomeranian, again.
Listen to this ad, *Champion bloodlines,*
girls, one orange, one tan, $200.
Cool, I can learn how to show and breed her.

I sure hope she didn't come from
a North Dakota Amish puppy farm.
She won't be a brat like my first pom.
Cremora hated being left alone while we worked.

When you scooted Cremora with the broom,
she got even and left her tooth marks,
like a nervous accountant's pencil
the day before the annual audit.

And, yes, she shredded the seats of our dining
room chairs when we locked her in the kitchen.
Forget about the chewed up Harley Davidson
boots and black leather belt in your closet.

You're going to San Angelo Tech school
while I stay with Mom and Dad for four months,
and Dad doesn't mind. I really want the cream
colored one. Please, say yes. Pretty please.

This is different. Mom and Dad will agree.
They'll say yes and will enjoy her, too.
It will be okay, so long as I take care of the dog.
Thank you, thank you. I love you.

I can't find the ad. The Journal tears. There.
Please be home. I can't breathe. Yes, yes.
We can be in New Underwood before six-thirty.
Darn. She already sold the cream one.

II.

The orange one might be okay. Dad drives
the van. That's got to be the house, the blue
colonial with a chain link fence. Look,
she's so tiny, such a serious bark.

She wears her puppy fur, in soft fuzzy fluff.
The tawny brown looks almost brindle,
with black streaks in her tail and back. I know
she'll change colors twice this year.

The breeder's sure she'll be orange sable like
her father. Foxy Johnny looks like a stocky fox,
with a friendly grin. Princess Pamee's
vanilla fur sticks to her worn body.

Both parents are locked in the house, so I
focus on the puppy. She charges at
me, barks, and runs away. She'd easily
carry the Ms. Independence award.

I chase her around the breeder's yard.
The puppy weighs nothing to scoop up.
Tucked inside Dad's baseball cap,
she curls up and smiles contentment.

She wiggles to be put down and follows
the granddaughter, to pick up her chip crumbs
and bubble gum. Her tail wags her sideways.
She plops down, but cocks her head to watch us.

I'm already in love, but remember
to ask for the genealogy. The breeder
fumbles, can't find it, but promises to
bring it to me at work when in town next.

I pretend I recognize Pomeranian
Champion names in her bloodline.
I just can't leave her one more night.
I hand over Dad's lent two-hundred dollars.

III.

I hold a bonus can of rich dog food
and cuddle my new love. Dad teases
how much per ounce I paid for her.
We speed down the interstate.

She squirms free and sniffs the van floor.
A terrible stench presses my nose.
Dad squeals brakes to the shoulder.
We comb the car. I swear she didn't poop.

I deposit orange fluff in the ditch
to do whatever. It was gas. Good Lord.
We all stand in the ditch and breathe.
Newlyweds take longer to break wind.

Next stop, Rushmore Mall pet store.
My new puppy needs paraphernalia.
I resist naming her Stinky,
and christen her Cinnamon.

Written in 1992

Popcorn

You microwaved popcorn. I thought
you were sweet to offer the bowl to me.
You turned and gave it away to another.

Not so bad a deed on the surface,
except your smirk. I knew you
were just being mean and spiteful.

It wasn't the first or only time
you showed me your ignoble side.
I confronted you before you asked

for a divorce punctuated with your fist.
I sadly agreed, reluctantly at first,
then tasted and enjoyed popcorn singly.

Written in 1995

Prairie Dog Native

Not as solid as Mt. Rushmore
nor changeable as dusty winds,
prairie town burrows
intertwine our social tunnels.
Black Hills shadow
many prairie dog towns
where we'll entertain you.
Summer heat swells
our fossilized sea bottom,
soon overcrowded with visitors
from Wall Drug or the Corn Palace.
Badlands is a misnomer.
This land is great,
except rattlesnake bites,
harsh blizzard endurance,
or inexperienced trail riders
occasionally trip in our holes.
Remember, we are way cuter
than any stuffed jackalope.
South Dakota has many little, but
great faces in great places.

Posted online on Poetic Asides *2009*

Preacher Said

Preacher said,
"Saved by grace."
Grandpa said, "Not true:
Works are what we need to do."
Little Tommy said,
"Grace, our horse, saves us
from walking."

Written in 2010

Problem with the USA

The United States of America unified?
Not on any one policy: political or national,
medical or financial, rural or urban,
environmental or industrial, federal or local.
Categorized into narrow groups: ethnic, gender, age,
brothers and sisters squabble for Uncle Sam's attention,
but defend against outsiders, even unto death.
Our citizens are individualized,
diverse from our collective parts.
Yet we are all respect-seeking Americans
united for the right to exist as a complete nation.

Posted online on Poetic Asides *2009*

Progressively Worse

First snow of winter:
Snow is amazing,
      hard and crunchy under foot,
      or so soft it won't stick
      a snowball together.

January snow:
Snow is unromantic,
      cold and slippery,
      sneaky drifts move
      in the middle of the night.

Snow is ugly:
      sticky and yellow
      muddy slush slicks on the
      bottom of my car.

I hope this is the last snow of Spring.

Written in 2008

Pruning Rose

Roses thrive with careful pruning,
send out shoots a foot longer than the ones cut off.
Then their blossoms blush with a youthful newness.

With my doctors' help, cancer pruned me.
They stripped away my control,
and attempted a complete removal of my dignity.

They replaced my once noticeable femininity
with long scars and promised to rebuild my breasts
after my physical healing was complete.

But proud, I stand with the Amazons, who chose
similar transformation for better archery skills.
I am readied to fight for my life with chemotherapy.

I endure side effects and digestive discomforts.
People say I look good in spite of skin blemishes.
Even on my worst days, my husband takes care of me.

Today my crown is devoid of hair. My friend and I cry.
I'm not ready for my world to view a GI Jane style.
She encourages me to shop for feminine sassy hats.

I am not strong. I am not brave.
I am a survivor, who refuses to hide.
God pruned me. He expects I will blossom more fully.

Written in 2010

Public Forum

Dedicated to FanStory.com

Fan-tastic e-publishing experience,
available for daydreams and
nightmare world creations.
Sensual and sometimes sensible,
telling stories, pen moving,
original poetry. Learn by
contemporary's reviews.
FanStory.com never filling,
but fully addictive.

Published on FanStory.com *in 2008*

Pulling Teeth

Papaw loves teeth.
Those hard, slick
and most durable
give him grief.

Look at his own
blackened choppers
from chewing tobacco
since he was half-grown.

Grin, spit. He fiddled,
to string small molars
between long sharp incisors
through holes he whittled.

Keen demand for his necklaces
at the summer fairgrounds.
Beaver and skunk teeth
often wanted in some places.

Posted on Poetic Asides *in 2009*

Puppy Yawn

Only a puppy could yawn
so big that he would knock
himself over backwards and
still come back smiling.

1977 Written for Creative Writing class at DWU

Pure Raindrops

Did you hear the rainstorm last night?
Each drop fell into suicide,
got saturated, lost in mud.

Purity is like a raindrop.
Each prism reflects rainbow light,
mists, then absorbs into mainstream.

2008 1ˢᵗ Place PST Annual Mid-South Festival and published in Tennessee Voices Anthology 2008-09

Puttin' On Weight

I've had a lot of years
to put on weight.
Weight of slights,
of hurt feelings,
of pain and disappointment.

I wrapped each cell
with fat to cushion
and protect me
from you, from myself,
from those
I foolishly trusted.

Written in 2010

Quiet

a Quintaine form

Quiet
is hard for me.
So much needs to be said.
Words explode in my tiny brain.
Relieve my pressure. Let me speak to you.

1977 Written for Creative Writing class at DWU

Quiet, Please

I'm enjoying the sun on my back deck.
The robin glares at me,
before she returns to feed
her nest full with peepers.

The world refuses to be hushed
for their new life struggles.
Each baby opens a wide mouth,
hopes for fresh food delivery.

Cars and motorcycles
roar past maple trees,
radios blare,
people argue.

Bluebirds sing, call
to their mates, warn
intruders, stake a
birdhouse claim.

Birds long for
quieter times in
lonelier neighborhoods
and quieter naps.

Quiet zones are ignored
everywhere. No place is
home to silence. Golden
are rare hushed moments.

Posted on Poetic Asides *in 2009*

Quilt

a Haiku form

Decorative and
warm, quilting is a lost art.
Find comfort again.

1985 published in Adventures in Quilting,
a how-to hand-quilt book based on Evelyn Rose's methods
and used in her quilting classes for beginners

Quilting Creation

Blue, red, yellow
diamonds, triangles, squares
violet, orange, green
four-patch, nine-patch, over-all pattern
borders, sashes, and strips
prints, stripes, dots
top, batting, and backing
quilting thread, needle and thimble
ruffles, self-binding or bias
A quilt is born with precise decision making.

Published 1985 in Adventures in Quilting

Rain Falls

a related Haiku form pair

Rain falls - drip, drop, drip,
light as transparent web silk.
Ancestors arrive.

Neighbors join mud dance.
Rain sprinkles renew dry chi.
Young dreams release love.

Written in 2009

Rainbows End

Today, all my rainbows end.
My path crosses the ocean,
pushes past my drowning fear.
Birds startle at brilliant hues.
They know my final ending
is where clouds hover.
Cliffs wall the next world.
I hope for the place I dread.

Will clouds disburse?
Will paths be easy?
Will rainbow colors
follow into the mist?
Will I cross the water
or trudge my usual rocky way?
Will I drown or breathe
freely of spiritual air?

I've reached many rainbow endings.
One finished when I graduated,
another when I wed, when my sons were born,
when I became the eldest family member.
Today is another graduation
from life's school. Will I return
to learn again what I've already forgotten?
Will I be welcome in the glorious kingdom?

2008 published on FanStory.com

Rainspout Drips on Lawn

pair of Haiku

Rainspout drips on lawn,
puddles stone birdbath,
finches' cheep-gossiping pool.

Lonely icy spout
now craves songbird company
vacationing south.

*2009 3rd Place, PST Annual Mid-South Poetry Festival
and 2010 second haiku published in* Grandmother Earth
Volume XVI

Reaching Out

Reaching out, I reached up,
hoped Mother would take my hand.

Making new friends in a strange town
when I was homesick, stretched my shyness.

Reaching out is touching your hand,
as I watch you look at me and smile.

I'd reach inside out if only
you would reach out to love me.

Written in 1972

Recession Obsession

Economic merry-go-round:
huge deficit,
minimal budget cuts,
congressional raises,
government furloughs
tax cuts versus tax hikes.

Less wages, equals
less taxes, equals
more deficit, equals
less wages, equals
less taxes, nets
more deficit.

Vote around Congress.
Veto from Oval Room.
Despair throughout
the country.
Cut, cut, cut, but
raise congressional wages.

Balance the budget,
close enough
for government work.

Written in 1990

Red-Hatter Anniversary

Riverfront Seafood's rough-planked banquet tables
hosted a sea of red-hat celebrating ladies this April 25th.
Each red-hatter sprouted a purple feather,
neck-wrapped a boa, or made statements
in other purple accessories.

Don't point and laugh at their garish red/purple wear.
Grin, but don't encourage their middle-aged
shenanigans. One hatter daintily removed gloves
before whomping a crab and splattering Old Bay
all over the brown paper tablecloth.

The ladies enjoyed a boisterous laugh, pretended
dress-up, and made-believe in their own high-society
almost anywhere. No red-hatter competes with their
pearl-wearing queen. No minutes are taken,
nor any agenda discussed except fun.

You'll spot them at plays, in restaurants, and lounges.
As for me, I'm having pink-hatter fun
in my lavender shift. I shan't admit I'm fifty yet.
I just want to know where to meet for the next
social event with my new red-hatter friends.

2008 Honorable Mention (from two judges) PST Annual Mid-South Poetry Festival and published in 2010 Lost State Voices, Volume III

Refocused

a SCOT form

Once, I thought I knew my purpose.
I felt my soul's one road was clearly marked.
Feeding fears with doubts, you drove me crazy.
I learned to choose my own best path.

2nd Place in the May 2012 PST monthly contest

Reincarnation

Past is present and future came.
First is second; the third's a game.

Restoration to a new dawn,
visions of what was are not gone.

Present, future, and past is done.
Second is third and first is spun.

Who are you and what do you do?
I'm nobody, now that I'm through.

Future, now. Renewal, begun.
Third, infinity. Past, rerun.

I am here and I didn't fall.
I've come back to seek my call.

Written in 1967; 1989 Won 3ʳᵈ place
at Central States Fair, Rapid City, South Dakota

Relationship Mistakes

Mistakes are many,
remedies few.
Chances are, many
are in love with you.

Jump too soon,
a fatal mistake.
Rush too soon
to a painful break.

Take time,
relax and enjoy.
Save time
for one special boy.

Written in 2009

Reluctant Service

Draft dodger,
not a name
he embraced.
Preferred airman,
though he didn't fly.
Avoided unpalatable
Viet Nam destination.

Technical high school
didn't prepare him for
boot camp Drill Sergeant's
latrine queen tag
for his spotless cleaning.

At a Montana SAC base
he earned Tech Sergeant,
serviced missile site electronics.
Rarely did they serve
lunch, except packed K-rations.

Mail slot collected dust.
No one sent fruit cake
or care packages.
He grew bored,
volunteered to serve
tour in Korea.

Not a choice to support war
except through forced enlistment.
He will not stand up on Veterans Day,
and said, "Don't honor me. I did my duty,
went home got on with my life.
Thank you very much."

Written in 2012 to Poetic Asides *PAD prompt (from a veteran's viewpoint)*

Remaining

In one short moment, my positioning
zoomed from the baby of my family
to sitting at the head table as the eldest
representative for my son and nephews.
Mom, Dad and older brother all died and
left messy paperwork and finances behind.

I couldn't defer to their expert opinions.
I became the point person for discussions,
presented a knowledgeable mature image
and pretended I knew all the correct answers
to the hardest life questions about death,
burial, taxes, monuments, and survivorship.

At first, it was unique to feel I was
the oldest in our family group.
It gave me a certain confidence.
I held my head up and acted
as a matriarch giving advice
to those younger and less wise.

Soon, like all survivors,
I experienced, what you,
who went before us,
already learned first-hand.
I know it's extremely sad
to remain here without you.

Written in 2009

Repression

The world staring in
my window was smudged.
My view was inside out.
I blamed the passing
cars for my confusion.

Each day was dull.
The streaks got worse.
Where was my sunshine?
When would he appear?
He left without a word, went
anywhere away from me.

My depression hole was deep.
My eyes were lakes
of the tears
I might as well shed.
No one will see.

I stare inside my world,
wipe the fingerprints away.
Outside is sunshine.
The gray world
passed my door.
Whether he returns or not,
I shan't care.

The paths are bright
with fallen leaves.
Their crunch awakens
a new rhythm.
I am not my window,
no longer streaked.
My view is
outside in.

Written in 1979

Rescue

I was living on the edge
when I fell into the pit.
I almost drowned in self-pity.

I looked up at you standing
with your hand out.
You tugged and pulled
me from the depths.

I smiled. Your eyes glowed.
All I said was "Thank you.
Thank you!"

Written in 1985

Retiring Labor Relations

How much is
ENOUGH
time + money + energy?

Computed, typed, filed
>for others.

When is it
MY
time + money + energy?

Answered, planned, decided
>for others

watched – waited = wasted
again and again.

ENOUGH
saving
my time + my money =

my energy,
NOW!

2005 recorded on The Sound of Words

Ride Metro and Relax

Washington, DC

Monday:
I take my noon stroll on
Columbus Circle toward the Capitol.
I see, *Ride Metro and Relax*,
displayed on the repair truck. I smile.
Monday evening, when I meet my husband,
I tell him. We laugh. Then he reminds me
for the rest of the week I need to ride Metro.

Tuesday:
Union Station, I am glad to see
the Red Line to Shady Grove waits for me.
Amid growls and sight daggers, I squeeze in.
My heels are still in the doorway.
My eyes beg to come aboard before the door
crushes my shoes and bites off my butt.
They give me a quarter inch.
I make it be enough.
We're all lumped together
like chunky tomatoes in pasta sauce,
when I learn they'd been stalled for twenty minutes.
Two impatient or claustrophobic managers bail out.
The latecomers think we made room for them.
Avoiding the elbow jabs, I say, "So sorry, " to the man
who demanded I not step on his briefcase.
I suppress a sneeze. I'm wondering,
How else will I get to my Poem-a-Day class?

Just before I resign, the driver says,
"The switching problem at Farragut North is remedied.
We'll be moving shortly."
We jerk and bump and stop midway between stations.
This is worse than when I started at Union Station.
Now, I'm a tired swimmer in the middle of the lake.
Ridiculous for me to turn back.
I must swim to the other side.
The train throws us forward into each apologetic other.
Finally, we get full electricity and steam between stops.
My fingers cramp around the standing pole.
Jerk, bump, stop, forward, jerk, bump, stop.
We're all tapping out a new dance step
to the rhythm of the train.

"Excuse me." I used to be good at following,
but then, the music was better.
After two station stops,
I'm able to maneuver into a close seat.
My personal space is so narrow today;
I feel like the crowd is in my lap.
The farther we go the fewer passengers.
I take a deep breath, avoid brushing anyone.
I relax and open my book. Then I hear,
"Bethesda." That's my stop.

2005 recorded on The Sound of Words

Right

You were right
to leave me
to grow up.

My world understanding
was learned the hard way.
Hard lessons are most memorable.

Thank you
for allowing me
space and time.

Written in 2012 for Poetic Asides *PAD prompt (right)*

Right of Way Relinquished

The train blew three blasts
to clear the city's intersection.

Collision crashed train to car.
Immovable object clashed obstinate intruder.

Siren screamed, screeched through traffic,
raced time to rescue residents.

1977 Written for Creative Writing class at DWU

Risky Business

I.

Rejection slips sit shuffled and stacked
near dog-eared market books with
publications scratched through all but
those who haven't yet rejected me.
No, no, no. I repeat my mantra.
They've rejected my work, not me.
My poems don't fit their needs for now.
My friend says her gambling
is much more profitable.

II.

"You can't make money
without spending money," she says.
I watch her play Keno bonus rounds
and kick myself for not investing
in the first five games. I keep track
of numbers for two hours, I don't write
a word. I'm confused. She spent forty,
won twenty-nine, and felt good.
She was only out eleven dollars.

III.

Eleven dollars? In less than two hours!
I would have gone to the bookstore,
read another poetry anthology,
bought socks, a Reuben sandwich,
or subscribed to a journal. I hit my head.
Eleven dollars buys a lot of stamps,
paper and ink. I'll gamble on poetry.
One day, I'll win. I will, I'm sure.
Watch for me in print or I'll die trying.

Written in 2004

Roaring Twenties

a Villanelle form

I.

Smack the competition. Amuse the goons.
Godfathers and tough thugs have a belief.
Keep police busy chasing those loons.

II.

Performers trumpet jazz speakeasy tunes,
leave the night with tips amid relief.
Smack the competition. Amuse the goons.

III.

A new diva gasps, faints and then swoons.
Rich widows pretend to be in their grief.
Keep police busy chasing those loons.

IV.

Bodies sometimes float in lagoons.
Butcher shops carved more than prime beef.
Smack the competition. Amuse the goons.

V.

Moonshine arrests for drinks in saloons.
Fear was served up as an aperitif.
Keep police busy chasing those loons.

VI.

News was blasted over city Tribunes,
overshadows sins of common thief.
Smack the competition. Amuse the goons.
Keep police busy chasing those loons.

Written in 2009

Roller Coaster Love

Climb up higher and higher.
      Go over the top.
Rush to the bottom.
      Start over.
Begin the ride again.

Written in 1989

Romantic Interlude

You took me through a storm.
My heart continues to thunder.
I ground on wooden planks.
What happened, love?
My fingers stroke my solar plexus.
Whew. I'm fully intact.

Crystals, please rejuvenate
my chakras, erase my base shame.
Take away my lust for
who was here and gone.
Wished for excitement came
but left with uneven calm.

Published on FanStory.com *in 2008*

Rooted

How many rose bushes have we planted
in the twelve married years?
We planted them and moved.
Someone else enjoyed. Not this time.
I want to stay here until I die or just can't
move on my own. I hope these rose bushes
love living with me as much as I love them.

Written in 2011

Roots, Leaves, and Thorns

Roots, leaves, and thorns.
You are nothing
until you bloom.

Written in 2002

Rose Cemetery

Pedro, South Dakota

I know of a place that's no place.
It's prairie and sky and grass that's dry.
Fences surround those who try to escape
a harsh life. Iron gate reflects the name,
Rose Cemetery. Homesteaded grounds
finalized family dreams for generations.

Written in 2004

Rose Dissected

I've looked at you now from all angles,
explored shadows and bright colors.
You sat in my vase for a day or two.
Hung upside down didn't save your color.
I sketched you. I photographed you.
I plucked you. I pulled apart your petals
and smelled each one as I placed
them in my potpourri. I still don't know,
why you are so special to me.
Maybe it's because we share a name.

Written in 2003

Rose Petals

a Haiku form

Rose petals windsurf.
Crickets call autumn cadence.
Thoughtful dreams decay.

2011 published in Grandmother Earth, Volume XVII

Rose's Other Names

a rose by any other name smells as sweet - Shakespeare

I've tried to be other than a Rose.
Anderson was too plain, too common.
Eatinger often mispronounced, too different.
Then there was Sultz, no not Shultz.
When I returned to my maiden name,
my mood was girlish and juvenile.
I added Klix, because he let me be myself
and not someone else's missus.

Written in 2003

Roses of Motherhood

I. *Like a Mother —one rose among many plants*
Myriad flowers surround a life.
Sunflower friends brighten us dawn to dusk.
Petunias are frosty survivors.
Marigold mentors, lilac models
choke poor example dandelions.
One blooming rose is admired the most,
not from birth, but also life-giving.
Thank you for your free guidance.

II. *New Mother —a rosebud*
Moments ago, just a young green bud,
barely showed color. Yet new life
sprouts inside you with sunshine and tears.
Heavenly rain droplets glisten leaves,
help you grow. Learn patient love.
Need to be a good example,
but learn fast for your new seedling.
Thank you for always doing your best.

III. *Practicing Mother —an opening blossom*
The shaded hues of blossoms defined
tentatively opened petals.
Study parenthood, during sleepless
worry nights. Each day is a pop quiz.
Teacher, friend, guide, all this even more.
Spring and summer are gone in a flash.
Crazy world explorers seek safe shade.
Thank you for your wisdom and advice.

IV. *Empty Nest —full bloom*
Seeds in the wind, years and children gone,
sought their own sunshine and felt their rain.
They didn't take root, not here, not now.
Lighthouse safe-haven perennial,
your fertilizer is tried and true.
Tenderness and training cling to them.
Sometimes they asked. Sometimes they listened.
Thank you. You know when to let go.

V. *Grandmother –dropping petals*

You're hardy and survived harsh winters.
Some thorny years have taken their toll.
Time for rocking chair philosophy.
Soft petals have started to wrinkle.
Hugs, kisses, love are miles away.
The scent of your perfume lingers.
It seems you will always be there, but . . .
Thank you for reaching out with your love.

VI. *Gone, Not Forgotten –potpourri and ashes*

Rain lasting throughout the quiet spring.
Fondly remembered good time smiles,
small events, warm and cuddly sunshine.
Your ashes are part of the good earth.
Gone away, but your essence stayed.
Your seeds and their seeds display unique hues.
So much like you, though they deny it.
Bless you for watching over them still.

2003 published in a Mother's Tribute – *Mother's Day 2003 at*
Holy Cross Lutheran Church, Greenbelt, Maryland and
2012 last stanza used as a dedication to the editor's grandmother
in Common Ground Herald

Rummage Sale Rummy

For my father Harmon Lee Rose July 12, 1919 to October 1, 2001

Whether an offer of hidden pleasure
or to show off the junk,
rummage sales are full of us.

Dad marked the ads, sign gazed,
mapped out the best neighborhoods,
right, then left. Often he turned around.

At a stop sign, he followed directional arrows.
He'd spot the colonial white house or
preferred the crumbling brick ranch-style.

Scout for saved treasure,
he acted polite and joked
as he rummaged through rubbish.

This bargain trailblazer
announced on his bumper sticker,
"I'm a Rummage Sale Rummy."

Written in 1992, 2012 placed as Tennessee State Senior Poet
Honor Scroll Award finalist and published in Senior Poet
Laureate's Golden Words

Running on Empty

an Epigram form

E Does Not Equal Enough.
This frequent fuel-saving bluff
drives me nowhere fast,
off track, out of gas.

Written in 2011

Rustic Barn

Framed by trees,
a rustic barn stands.
What is inside?
Dare I look?

2008 Published in Barn Charm *chapbook*

Rustic Repose

an Acrostic form

The hike up the hill
Always brought thoughts of
Super tasting plums
That we picked and brought
Every fall to can.

To feel the smooth stones
On the path, had made
Users feel unsure.
Coarse tree trunks scratched, but
Helped us stay upright.

Stupendous vistas
Invited returns.
Grand panoramas
Had awesome effects.
Treasures we enjoyed.

Stimulating scents
Met our noses. The
Early smells of day
Lingered in the grass, with
Lists of pungent odors.

High on the hill, we
Echoed our voices,
Answered tenors
Rang through the trees and
Interrupted the
Noiseless calm of the
God-loved scenery.

1977 Written for Creative Writing class at DWU

Salem, Mass.* Hysteria

February 1692 to May 1693

Reverend Samuel Parris tired of hearing
his daughter Betty and niece Abigail's complaints
of boredom. He was too busy overseeing his
parishioners' public penance for many perceived
societal slights or religious infractions. Puritans played
no games, celebrated no holidays; life was too serious
for childhood. But Betty and Abigail delighted in
listening to their slave Tituba's tantalizing tales about
voodoo practices, sexual encounters with demons, and
fortune telling.

Stir in the Salem witch's caldron: Putnam and Porter
family feuds, religious strictness, property disputes, and
a time when supernatural elements were blamed for
infant deaths, crop failure and assorted village troubles.
The girls' fits of rolling on the ground, body contortions.
the strange sounds baffled the doctor's examination.
They were not epileptic seizures nor of any natural
disease. Reverend Parris attributed the strangeness
to witchcraft.

Encouraged by their power, the girls named those who
bewitched them. Those accused named others. One by
one magistrates arrested men and women for religious
prejudices, political, and personal reasons, conducted
interrogations, forced confessions, held trials, and
imprisoned over one-hundred-fifty people using
spectral evidence. In the tiny crowded witch's dungeon,
high tide pulled water into their minute cells. Prisoners
stood knee deep in sea water and their own feces.

Property and assets were seized. Some family members
paid support fees and supplied the only food and
clothing provided the shackled prisoners. By hanging,
authorities executed, fourteen women and five men, cut
them down, and threw their bodies into a shallow grave.
Relatives secretly reburied them on private property.
At least five more perished in prison. Giles Corey
refused to plea to the court. He was crushed to death by
piling more and more heavy rocks on his chest.

The hysteria spread to neighbor towns where the girls
and other accused were unsuccessful in identifying
witches. When the girls pointed their fingers at the
Governor's wife, they'd gone too far. He declared an end
to the trials. The forced penniless prisoners languished
until jail fees were paid. A few pardons were given.
Many legal, religious, moral, and psychological issues
surfaced, but the most frightening lesson remains:
Beware of bored teenagers.

*original abbreviation for Massachusetts

Written in 2011

Salute and Honor

Fly high on top the building.
Touch the young girl's heart.
Caress the soldier's coffin.
We now see you everywhere.

Flap on the car windows and antennas.
Twirl on the kite's tail and wind sock.
Grace each proud person's window
and salute from airbase and dock.

Whether worn or flown,
folded or furled,
your colors are perfectly pure.
Your stars and stripes just right.
It's been our country's
lackadaisical cure.

Written in 2002

Saxophones and Jack Hammers

a Villanelle form

Saxophones and jack hammers competed
in DC Union Station's crowded corridors,
contrasted musicians with construction.

Creative songsters and audience greeted
contracted workers with muscular chores.
Saxophones and jack hammers competed.

Sweet songs set aside and jazz was bleated,
echoed, and slid across marble floors,
contrasted musicians with construction.

Neither one planned to become defeated.
Coins were released less for encores.
Saxophones and jack hammers competed.

As sweaty brows were overheated,
notes shouted and vibrations closed doors,
contrasted musicians with construction.

Lunch time toe-tapping not repeated,
energized electrified noise level soars.
Saxophones and jack hammers competed,
contrasted musicians with construction.

Written in 2004

Scott's Dots

a Limerick form

There once was a person named Scott,
who clipped out one gigantic dot.
He punched millions from just one
until he stacked up a whole ton
to be buried by dots and forgot.

Written in 1978

Seamless Closure at a Flea Market

Dedicated to my grandmother Jennie Grace (DeGeest) Swinehart
9 October 1897 – 15 December 1984

The gypsy dressed man
gathered fake pearls
and shiny tumbled rocks
from his cheesecloth bag
and then stirred them as they
clattered into a blue metal bowl.

I palmed a handful of stones
which took me back to playing
with my South Dakota Grandma's Mason jar,
brimful of multi-colored buttons:
tiny and huge, square and round.
Our family's Queen of Stitches recycled.

Shaking the jar, as a playful rattle,
another generation was entertained.
We played, button-button, who's got the button?
But knew Grandma harvested all our
old clothes fasteners. She continued to collect
from her children's children's children.

My cousin's navy uniform anchor
button rested at ease under glass.
She thimble-pushed black or white thread
to securely reuse a bone button
cut off Grandpa's worn-out work shirt.
Then she sewed it onto his flannel jacket.

This careless granddaughter
was saved an empty buttonhole
with lessons of stitches.
Once, Grandma asked me,
why a trashed sock wasn't darned.
I said, "Darn you, sock."
She was not amused.

The flea market vendor asked,
"Aren't they beautiful?"
My memories grinned. I relived
forgotten times and unraveled memories
rattling inside Grandma's button jar.

Written in 2004

Seasonal Artist

Leaves cling, but become
crimson, brassy, or gold.
They choose to adjust colors
like seasonal attitudes.
With missed cloaks, they envy
the steadfast square-needled spruce.

Our Creator streaks paint
to color hillside paths.
Denuded trees shiver winter,
nap to dreams of warm beams.
Evergreens stand sentinel,
uphold white blankets.

God, The Artist,
deprives trees of sugar
they gobbled all summer.
Green disappears except
from diabetic evergreens.
They change for no one.

Written in 2010

See a Rose

crisp bright petals
soft pastel buds

monarch butterfly
pollination rest stop

five fringed leaves
green stems climb

thorns prick
you back to reality

see a rose
think of me

2005 published in Schrom Hills Park *chapbook*
and 2008 in Barn Charm *chapbook*

Seed and Ant

An ant pushed the sunflower seed
under my seat at Seabrook's Metro station stop.
I pondered on helping, but didn't know his plan.
Train arrived. I boarded. Guilty thoughts remained,
because I did not assist the creature's struggle.

I shrugged. Probably I would frustrate him more.
He didn't request my interference. Pensively, I prayed.
God is much smarter than I in ant and human matters.
Perhaps He wants me to work out my own ideas, but
waits for prayers before He helps me interpret my life.

Written in 2004

Shadow, My Black Cat

Only the Shadow knows
     how lonely and desperate I was.
Only the Shadow needed me
     and hated to admit that.
She paced the floor when I was gone
     and ignored me at our home.

Shadow didn't like the boy friend
     I thought I loved, intended to marry.
Only she knew his authentic character.
     She warned me in her own way,
batted his head. He swatted her.
     I found Shadow another home.

I listened to my heart and not to my cat.
     I kept the wrong one and lost them both.

Written in 1988

Signature

It's a *don't bother me* signature
just as illegible as can be.
No one will know to whom to respond.

She said her piece and
clearly didn't want a reply.
The sentiment sang out.

Freely anonymous,
the letter writer released burdens
to be recycled in a compost pile.

Themes, feelings, hurts stacked up
against avoidances and compromises.
Life's balancing acts for humanity.

Write in code. Keep it vague.
Be abstract. Never reveal your
inner feelings with concrete words.

My neighbor's aunt, red-faced,
claimed no knowledge of such things
revealed by written specificity.

Her signature voice
tripped her penned tongue
into showing her identity.

Written in 2004; 2009 Honorable Mention in
PST Annual Mid-South Poetry Festival

Silence

It's been a long time,
since I could listen
to the pure silence.

Written in 1974

Silly Smiley Face

You are only a smiley face
on a shopping bag,
thrown to the curb as litter.
There you sit grinning at me,
will me to respond.
You still intrigue me.
I can't help but smile back.
Isn't that silly?
Oops, my light's changed.
See ya.

Written in 2003, 2007 published in Open Hearth

Simply Salad

You deny art appreciation, and say,
  "The Smithsonian is filled with junk."
Yet, I admire your
  carefully torn, crisp lettuce.

Cucumber slices stood in the bowl's circle,
  grape tomatoes and black olives
dotted their pattern,
  like red and black electrical wires.

I smile at its delightful presentation.
  You frown as
I complicate it,
  add my own cheese, mushrooms, dressing.

I like how you grow more
  creative, teach me to be less complex.
I'm a struggling artist,
  bored, frustrated and afraid to quit my day job.

You are an electrician lighting
  museum pieces you profess not to appreciate.
We're not a stew,
  and don't blend each ingredient of our individuality,

but a simple symmetry,
  like a salad filled with unique tastes.

2004 original written in Rose Solari's Poem-A-Day class
at the Writers' Center in Bethesda, MD

Single

an Acrostic form

Single is being a complete person
In a world where marriage was prevalent.
No one should feel that they need to
Grope for someone to complement them.
Less emphasis is being placed on
Everybody becoming whole through marriage.

Written in 1987

Sleeping In

At last you've retired the
five o'clock alarm to make
your night longer, day shorter.
Aw! You slept 'til seven thirty.

You chose less money
and gained time for enjoyment.
Younger workers keep
your time clock. Go play.

Today you choose between
gym and golf, hoped to
garden before it rains.
Pay checks are vegetables.

Rich in minutes, you cut
your expenses. Enjoy life
as long as possible. Let's
spend the kids' inheritance.

Posted on Poetic Asides *in 2009*

Sleepy Mockingbird

a Haiku form

Sleepy mockingbird
trills heavy rapture wishes,
tips his saucy tail.

Written in 2011

Slow Down

a Concrete or Picture form

Time, a monstrous thief,
creeps up when I am
reminded to complete the
project before the crucial
deadline.   I'm lost in
another moment and
carelessly   hurry
through traffic.
It gives me
twenty – four
hours, laughs,
snatches
it back

minute
by
minute.

Even if
I lived
on the
dateline,
traveled
backward to
forward,   I
could not arrest
time to catch up
to itself, or stop
robbery of found
moments, when I didn't
make time to slow down.

2007 published in Open Hearth

Slowly Pitched

Treasured objects, retired from daily use,
rest quietly inside my china cabinet.
Stored near Great-Grandmother Minnie's painted china,
Grandma Jennie's alabaster doves, and my Cretan plate,
I found Rob's grazed, slow-pitch softball.

My husband always resents any and all offers of help
and never displays the slightest weakness.
In his sixtieth summer, he abandoned a favorite sport
as a silent protest over the highest insult,
his unnecessary replacement by a designated runner.

Inside a drawer, out of sight, his keepsake is preserved.
He wrapped the grass-stained ball with Mom's
crocheted doily, laid the scored sphere atop a tablecloth
embroidered with silver roses.
Memories of youth neighborhood games nestle
with his sports relic enclosed within our shared
cupboard of vintage reminiscences.

Written in 2009; 2011 Honorable Mention in
PST Annual Mid-South Poetry Festival

Smithsonian Tour

Washington, DC 2004

On my lunch break I toured the
Smithsonian Postal Museum
with many interesting
exhibits of pony express routes,
postal clerk windows,
historic postage stamps and
an office display with an
old manual typewriter.

It reminded me of my first black
Remington Rand before I was
introduced to the fast IBM
Selectric with correction tape.
I've technologically graduated
to write on a laptop.
While I reminisced, I waited
for the lady ahead of me.

She showed the relics to her
grandson. He pointed at the
typewriter, questioned
its purpose. She explained,
it was like a computer
in the olden days.
Wrinkled, this antique
shuffled back to work.

Written in 2009

Snapshot

an Ekphrastic form using a photographic image prompt

Unrecognizable words smeared.
Thoughts appeared once, but
now erased to chalk dust.

Questions came easy.
Criticisms piled simply.
Answers just didn't add up.

Smudges of chalk dust
transformed ideas
into unrecognizable smears.

Written in 1977 in DWU creative writing class

Snow

Snow is unromantic:
      cold and slippery,
      silently sneaks up
      at midnight.

Snow is not amazing:
      hard crunches
      or too soft
      for a snowball.

Snow is ugly:
      muddy slush,
      sticky and yellow
      on the car bottom.

Written in 1990

Snow Angels

a Heroic Couplet form

My sleepy town ignores the pealing bells.
The sun sends sparkles, shines on icy cells.
One Sunday morning's opportune display
reminds me not to waste a winter day.

I shiver, shake, relinquish spent dull sleep,
while quiet piles of snow become too deep.
As skittish birds desert the dawn for nests,
some flakes touch silent hints on honored guests.

My tired red eyes refocus, then I see
four angel spectacles in front of me.
An angel dances jazz on banks of snow.
Cute giggles ring my yard while fierce winds blow.

Those luminaries chase through goose-track spin.
They ski and slide, run over, slip, and win.
I sigh as their appearance fades away.
I must take care to clear the slush this day.

While bundled up, I scrape a lucid path.
I toss the snow but wish for snugly bath.
Alone, poor humans hold impatience flaws.
A snowy angel purely dreamt soon thaws.

2010 Honorable Mention PST Annual Mid-South Poetry Festival

Snow Birds

Fly north to Santa Claus,
tattle on misbehavior,
soar south to warm weather,
return to herald spring.
Snow birds are mythical creatures.

Nomads wander southwest deserts,
or motor home to winter in Florida,
brag about freedom to roam nationwide,
return when sunshine points north.
Snow birds are an American icon.

Written in 2009

Snow Blanket

A blanket of snow doesn't
feel warm and toasty on my toes.
I think of frostbite and
gangrene, not a comforter.

Snow banks don't hold
much money either.
They melt away and
reveal the stash.

Posted on Poetic Asides *2011*

Snowless Globe

Encased in glass,
lily blossomed in my hand.
Her silvered tips sparkled
when I twirled the globe.
Reflections rained colors
which could not reach her
from my tea cup or television picture.
The artist encased her with frozen bubbles
where they lived alone in their crystal space.
Time preserved her youthful innocence.
Petals remained virginal white,
protected from a world filled with color.
Her life only blooms when I turn her sarcophagus.

Written in 2012 in the Elizabeth Hunter class, Buffalo Mountain Workshop at East Tennessee State University (ETSU)

Snowy Spring

Harsh wind,
eastern blast
blows white
petal piles
in my patio corner.

Now Bartlett pear,
later dogwood,
then magnolias
not cold
odorless snow.

I'd rather receive
an April avalanche
of multi-colored petals
in Maryland than
a South Dakota snow drift.

Written in 2004

So, We Watched Both

The golf Masters and Detroit Dog Show on one TV.
We never learned how to picture-in-picture. During
lags and commercials, we channel back and forth.

Fans out-color Augusta's blooming azaleas.
Fifty contenders battle for green jackets.
Brown Bermuda greens, lush green fairways.

Treacherous woods, hazardous water,
tricky bunkers, plain old dumb luck,
added to professional skill and experience.

During your first bathroom break, I switch.
Detroit's fair and chilly forty-two didn't compare.
Suit jackets or skirts ran dogs around the show ring.

Sporting, Hound, Toy, Terrier ,
seven groups, judged within the breed.
Best of breed judged within its group,

Best of Show compared 200 classes:
hound competed Chihuahua,
St. Bernard against Scottish terrier.

TV control switched.
During our supper break,
we call a truce. Then back to

Detroit contenders:
Rhodesian Ridgeback and Dalmation.
Are out-cuted by a foo-foo Toy Poodle.

Best of show disappoints
my love of canines.
I relinquish any further control.

Looks like a three-way golf play-off.
Younger Campbell, older Perry,
and Argentinean.

We pick the forty-eight-year old
to master as the oldest winner.
Campbell might win another day.

Two way tie:
Perry and Cabrera at the last hole.
Argentinian wins the Masters this year.

Beautiful Easter day,
we watched TV on both
channels together.

Posted on Poetic Asides *2009*

So, Why do We have War?

If I ran the world,
there would be no war.
Or maybe there would be
more wars, because they
wouldn't agree with me.

How can we please all?
Everyone needs so much:
peace, love, respect,
food, clothing, shelter,
a future for the next generation.

I think we should talk it out,
be tolerant of each other,
and set our boundaries.
That's what you think, too?
So, why do we have war?

Written in 2004

Soldier

a Limerick form

There once was a soldier in barracks,
who spent his spare time rewriting lyrics.
He was then court-marshaled they say.
For rhyming words, he did pay
for the laughter caused by his jeer-icks.

Written in 2004

Some People

Some people
don't care what they say
into a cell phone, or
who's forced to listen.
They imagine their own
invisible phone booth.

Written in 2004

Something New Enters

I'm only a visitor for now
in the land of survivorship.
Each woman tells me her story
of when she discovered the intruder,
what her doctor did to kill it, and how
the pills continued to keep it away
for five years. They truly believe
the doctors know the right cure.

"Just do as your doctor says.
Keep a good attitude.
That will cure the cancer."
Is it a cure? Did they survive
the cancer or the treatments?
Are they lucky to have a pill
to swallow for only five years?
Could there be another way?

Many ways? God's ways?
Natural remedies? Prayers?
Healing energies? Nutrition?
Not fighting toxins with more toxins?
I've listened. I've read.
I've become confused.
Do I believe strong
enough to bet my life?

I created this lump,
this overactive reproduction.
I've stressed myself
and not listened to my body.
It was a small irritation
which is viewed as monstrous.
Can a loving energy retard it?

Posted on Poetic Asides *2009*

Soul, Body, and Mind

Balance

spiritual   physical
    mental   spiritual
        physical   mental

pray   worship
    floss   exercise
        meditate   relax

                    more care
                    less hurt
                    more love

spiritual   physical
    mental   spiritual
        physical   mental

Balance

2005 published in Faith and Spirit *chapbook*

Soundtrack of my Life

On family trips we sang.
Dad's *Cowboy Jack* song,
Girl Scout songs, school songs
78s, 45s, 33 1/3s CDs, IPod,
music store, Mom's ESP
picking out sheet music
for customers, violin practice.

My transistor radio tuned in
Wolfman Jack at KOMA radio
in Oklahoma City.
He introduced me to artists
every modern teenager loved.
Gene Pitney's romantic croons
and the Monkeys on the
"Last Train to Clarksville."
These were new friends and
I sorted out the ones I liked.

One day, on the school bus,
Terry sang out, "Elvis is dead.
Long live the Beattles."
Elvis dead? My new friend?
How do I mourn his passing?
Elvis hadn't died yet.
She meant a new kind of beat
moved center stage
in her music world.

2010 Written at a Jane Hicks workshop
sponsored by PST-NE

South Dakota Contrasts

You say you've never
known someone
from South Dakota. I say,
"They let a few of us escape."

It's a land of contrasts:
the prairie, hills, badlands,
Sturgis motorcycle rally,
Spearfish Corvette classic,

Corn Palace, Wall Drug
Mount Rushmore,
Cheyenne River breaks,
welcome all tourists.

They let many stay.
We will travel back.
It's a comfort to see
white spaces between towns.

Written in 2005

Southern Lady

should be read with an affected Southern accent

No one in my adopted Tennessee
dare tell me I'm not a southern lady.
Being born in one of the only two
authentic southern states, fully qualifies me.

For you see, in order for something
to be south, there must be something north.
Most born and bred southerners proudly point
to the divisive Mason-Dixon line.

Look, only South Carolina is absolutely,
hands down, south of North Carolina.
It even incorporates "south" in its
glorious name. That leaves just one other state.

Don't argue with me and say I'm not a
southerner. I'll tell y'all right now
that my birth state, South Dakota, is solidly
south of North Dakota. Therefore,

I fully qualify as a bona fide
southern lady just as much as my current
Appalachian neighbors, who like
to think of me as a transplanted Yankee.

'Sides, Great-Grandma was a Lee.

Written in 2009 and posted on Poetic Asides,
2011 published in Funny you should say that . .
and in Spring 2012 Pasque Petals *the SDSPS anthology*

Spirit of All

Spirit of truth,
      tell the miracles of God.
Spirit of grace,
      talk of salvation through Christ.
Spirit of knowledge,
      lecture the mysterious scriptures.
Spirit of God,
      speak with everlasting love.
Spirit of humanity,
      shout over daily noise.
Whisper your messages,
      Holy Spirit, spirit of all.

2003 published in The Way of the Cross

Spring Frolics

The Prince of
Serendipity lives
in a mirage which
refuses to dissipate
until turtle dreams
of June picnics appear.

Spring,
Mother Earth's daughter,
frolics, creates rainbows
with crocus, tulips,
and butterfly wings.

A maelstrom whirls
their destinies together.
Mother Earth's growl
cannot beckon Old Man
Winter before Spring
chooses her summer prince.

Published on FanStory.com *in 2009*

Spring Greening

Ah
Spring, my favorite season.
Ah Choo!
Daffodils and tulips arrive,
dogwoods bloom,
fresh mown grass.
Ah, ah, Choo!

Pollen covers my car.
Mmmm. Fresh air.
Petals blow all over
the garden mulch.
Ahhhh. Renewal time.

Cardinals chase each other,
shop for nest twigs,
drop berries on my window.
Frisky squirrels dig up bulbs.
Spring, my favorite season.
Ah Choo!

Written in 2005

Spring, March 20, 1979

The thermometer read below zero.
Denver's weatherman
calculated the wind chill.

Overnight, snow piled in front
of our apartment. We shoveled out
enough to reach carpool and school bus.

Later, hot chocolate warmed us up.
While macaroni boiled, I chopped cheese,
and we exchanged the day's news.

Today, sure didn't feel like
the first day of Spring.
My seven-year-old son said,

"God must have had a lot
of leftover snow, that He just
had to get rid of last night."

Written in 2011 at a Jane Hicks workshop
sponsored by PST-NE

Squeet and Twirly

Mother's quilt shop kept her super busy:
sewing, teaching and selling cloth she loved.
The hours flew past so fast. She was dizzy
with hunger for more of the time she once
shoved aside for active home and family.

Dad retired to yard work, supported her
hobby, turned career, she embraced fully.
Often he worked as her unpaid chauffeur.
Most days, at noon Dad called "Squeet."

When translated his line meant, "Let's go eat."
Mom, involved deep, often said "Twirly."
Not surprising, her reply, meant "Too early."
One clerk heard this exchange daily,
nicknamed Dad *Squeet* and Mom *Twirly*.

Written in 2009

Still Missing You

You laugh at me and
say I'm crazy.
You watch me cry and
try to help.
But do you really
know me?

You leave me, you
disappoint me,
and yet you say
you love me.
I wonder, do you really?

I hate the telephone
when you leave me alone.
When I want it to ring it can't.
It never tells me what I want to hear.
So stay near. Is that clear?

Written in 1970

Stitch by Stitch

Stitch by stitch and piece by piece,
your quilt will keep you warm.
Made of wool, flax or fleece.
Cotton or polyester blend is the norm.

Needles weave in and out, while you
dream about a gift to someone
or hope that a judge will see that you do
your quilting better than that one.

Written in 1985 for Adventures in Quilting

Stop Watch

Sit still.
Don't Move.
Don't Tick
Don't Tock.
Time, stay still!

Written in 2009

Storm

a Syllabic form

Storm,
tempest
cyclone, gale
scream, holler, shout.
Suppressed emotions
whirl, gather momentum,
tear up all the soft grassroots.
Promised rose garden blown away.

2009 1ˢᵗ Place and published on Fan Story.com

Strong Weaknesses

Only forty minutes would give me fright
in the wilderness with naught but hard stones.
From the devil You would not think to buy
a bite from a loaf, not even one grain.
Tempted for forty days and each their night.
For what? You knew they would break
Your bones for this wretched sinner.
You knew You'd die for me.
You still endured the suffering and pain.

Follow you? I haven't really tried, Lord.
I can't remember to concentrate long.
Disciples were shown transfiguration
and Your Father in heaven said, *Well pleased.*
I am too weak. I've long grown bored.
I fear to lose much. My faith is not strong
in this place with walls in a religious nation.
One day Your suffering will be appeased.

My daily struggles compared are nothing.
Lord, please don't give up on me.
From the temple, You may want to drive me out.
You know I am pathetic and weak.
I can't endure Your tremendous suffering.
My heart isn't hard. I don't make a fuss.
Lord, I plead for You to turn me about.
I try to listen when You speak.

Please give me hope and surround with love.
I need rest and relief from my burdens.
Lord, remind me. Put Your cross before me.
I see You, I know You, but I forget.
I want to dwell there in heaven above.
You always weep for Your weak ones.
Lord, show me majestic heaven and thus.
I'm sorry You paid for my sin-filled debt.

2003 published in The Way of the Cross

Suicide

Poets talking

"Sylvia Plath wrote this
while she was dying."

"She wasn't dying.
She killed herself."

"That's because
her spirit died."

Written in 2004

Summer Diamante

Summer
loveliness dies.
Autumn replaces it
with crisp settings and golden hues.
Sunshine stays, but cooler and more aloof.
Warm days are here for a short time then, poof!
South for the winter amid boos
of discontent. We sit.
I hate white lies.
Bummer!

Written in 2008

Summer Hangs Her Heavy Head

Sunflowers follow sun no more,
bow their heads for cardinal needs,
stand plucked clean of dried seeds.
The birds harvest and clearing chore.

Then ninety degrees was the norm.
Now replace petunias with mums.
Disquieted bumble bee hums.
Dried grass welcomes a thunderstorm.

Summer hangs down her heavy head.
She'll soon move to cool the climate.
Then we will see snow to mime it,
snuggle down deep inside our beds.

Published on FanStory.com *August 2008*

Sunday Matinee

A dollar to go
enjoy the show.
A dollar a seat,
whether big or neat.

1977 Written for DWU Creative Writing class

Sunrise at Cocoa Beach

Florida's east coast
prompted my desire
for an ocean sunrise.
I programmed my alarm.

Camera ready, we waited.
A chilly breeze tickled my hair.
In slow motion, gray sky
blossomed pink streaks.

Ocean steel waves
and white surf foamed,
answered a blue call
to reflect the spreading light.

Golden clouds watched
our proud tearful hug.
I smiled appreciation
as though our presence

here, together at this time,
willed the old sun to rise
over the ancient ocean
for one more glorious day.

Written in 2010

Surprise Gifts

Special packages
were on my wish list.

Patience topped my schedule
and opportunities appeared.

Unexpected deliveries
were tied with festive bows.

I accepted loneliness,
but love comforted me.

Smiles arrived to clear
my tear-stained heart.

I'm often thrilled
with life's surprise packages.

Written in 2008

Sweet Honey Song

Song Lyrics

Syrupy,
Sticky,
Gooey,
Sweet,
Honey is a
Bee-u-tiful treat!

It sticks to your fingers
and hangs on your tongue.
Swallow it down
to have some fun.

What it does to my body,
don't tell me, my dear.
To my hips, to my waist,
I pretend not to hear.

Syrupy,
Sticky,
Gooey,
Sweet,
Honey is a
Bee-u-tiful treat!

Written in 2009

Symbolic Cymbals

a Dorsimbra form

Louisa, not strictly sick, ended her
happy existence farce performances.
Dead marriage, suicidal wife deserved
cymbals, symbolic of grand finale.

piercing, jarring,
banging, clanging discs,
thought-snapping escape
from disconsolate courtesy

Cymbals, symbolic of grand finale,
jangle concrete lives, snub ethereal.
Widower Sam, did not practice melancholy,
but bought wife's noisome uncultured funeral.

Written in 2009

Take War, It's Yours

Yeah, Yeah, Yeah.
Even the news is in re-runs.
Talk is still about an Iraqi war
Mr. Bush ended more than a year ago.
Why are you still showing me
roadside bombings and hostages
pleading for their lives?

It's not my war. It was started
by a president and prime minister,
who didn't agree with a dictator.
They should face each other. Instead they call up troops.
Military leaders and generals like that sort of thing.
Soldiers knew when they signed up for education
that they could get called on for defense.

Iraq voted for their leader.
Leave them alone. It's their country.
Those we rescued don't appreciate
our continued involvement.
Leave me alone. It's your war.
You finance it. I didn't vote for it.
Let's have more comedy on TV.

Written in 2005

Taking Back

Every day,
every tide,
across sand, over rocks,
the liquid sea deposits shells
and shards she planned to take back.

Drop by drop,
inch by inch,
the sea trumps human desires
to hold whispered ambitions.
I beg for secure feet,

stand on stacked boulders,
push against tides. Hold fast
my floods of helplessness
and fully acquit
my unbound migration.

Perhaps more solid ground
lies inland with its own currents.
The hypnotic sea attempts to seize me,
swishes forward and aft.
She anchors me to this tenuous place.

Can I view her sculptures on the shoreline,
but accept compulsory adjustments?
I re-route my stubborn mind.
My feet release fear of an uncertain future.
I take back free will and move on.

Many shards and shells
deposited by this liquid sea
remain within me
every tide,
every day.

Written in 2009

Tattered Flag

T-shirt proclaims:
"These colors may bleed but they won't run."

Tattered, it flies proudly.
The wind has not defeated
this piece of cloth,
but so much more:
red for blood,
white for purity,
blue for fidelity.
The first thirteen striped states
and all the stars which followed.
Faded, but blazoned in my heart.

Written in 2002

Teetering on Homicide

Love, a balancing act,
teeters on emotions,
totters out of control.
With two we'll be level,
if we work together,
offsetting ups and downs.

Our teeter-totter sits
unbalanced. You leave me
up in the air, drop the ball
on our marriage.
When you leave with her
I fall hard to the ground.

I contemplate murder, but
hers, or yours, or both?
Mixed thoughts swing
between painless poison
or a serrated knife.
Blood is a sticky clean-up.
I want to relish your suffering.

Love is out of control.
Negativity rules.
No, no, no - No, no, no
Return happy endings.
Stop these horrible plans.
Calmly divorce without violence.

Age was my sin.
Youthful companion
satisfies your ego.
In time, she may understand.
Your lies are not her fault.
I believed you once too.

No need to scream
on a roller coaster ride.
I want stability. Demand respect.
Go ahead. You deserve each other.
Why spoil two families?
Have a good life.
I'll put away the knife.

Written in 1995, published on FanStory.com *2009*

Temper Temper

a Triolet form

A temper flares until dust settles
      where tension coughs and chokes
life from everyone like prickly nettles.
A temper grows until dust settles.
      Anger steams when someone meddles.
Infuriation simmers and smokes.
A temper lasts until the dust settles
      where emotion coughs and chokes.

1977 Written for DWU Creative Writing class;
2009 won 3rd Place in PST Annual Mid-South Poetry Festival

Temptations

a Cinquain form

Roasted
ears, toasted nuts,
claim this victim once more.
She swallows difficult words like
Diet!

Published on FanStory.com *in 2009*

Tennessee Adoption

Spirits stand guard
over tiers of life.
God-layered mountains.
Deep hollers, brim
with wildflowers and dew.

I deep-breathe solace,
inhale, exhale. Listen.
Birds gossip. Squirrels tattle.
We climb rocky trails
to spot views of strata.

I wander far to hear
the lonesome wind whisper.
Retire from stress
in our autumn gold mist.
Appalachia, adopt me,
fortress my mountain home.

Written in 2009

Thanksgiving 1974

Erik sat at the end
of the six-foot dining table addition.
Whipped cream was out of tongue reach
on his chubby cheek.

His two-year-old eyes
catalogued all the dishes:
roasted turkey, mashed potatoes,
cranberry sauce, pumpkin pie.

He sighed, took a deep breath,
sighed again and again.
His eyes wanted more.
His tummy was tightly packed.

Everyone else finished and left.
He wouldn't, or couldn't, move,
but smiled at the celebration spread,
and sighed and sighed.

Written in 2012 to a PST-NE November meeting
prompt (favorite holiday memory)

Pastiche of Poetry

Thermos

Thermos,
warm chocolate
traps cocoa in milk
to be released on my taste buds.
So good!

1977 Written for DWU Creative Writing class

Thin Promise

I asked when my hair
would fall out.
She said, "It might get thin."

Maybe my cancer
treatments would not
kill all my hair follicles.
For two days I brushed,
pulled out a few loose strands.
My balcony's wind carried
the filaments across
the sports bar parking lot.

Maybe I won't need a wig or
be expected to cover a bald head
with a slippery scarf.
Maybe it won't be so bad.
A week later, I shampooed almost
all my hair onto the shower drain.
Each time my hand touched
my once thick cap of hair,
a fistful let loose.

I screamed. I cried.
I felt betrayed.
I thought I was exempt.
Thin? My foot! I was bald.
She gave me false hope
and I was not prepared.

Written in 2011

Three Tanka

Rose petals
wind surf as crickets
call autumn,
and I dream about
decaying delicately.

My turbulent thoughts
equaled dirty laundry loads
you memory scrubbed,
bleached with friendly forgiveness,
erased misplaced stained thoughts.

Mockingbird's
sleepy song trills heavy,
rapture wishes.
He tips his saucy tail
and dances with Spring.

Written in 2011

Through the Needle's Eye

Needles Highway, Black Hills, South Dakota

Miles away, high in the Black Hills,
among the Cathedral Spires,
where tunnels frame
Mount Rushmore,
I often take deep cleansing breaths,
envision a rock formation,
and meditate on the Needle's Eye.

My brother Jim and I
didn't see eye-to-eye, ever
in my childhood memories.
We spent decades apart.
The year our father was sick,
I needed a break from the hospital,
and begged Jim to take me
on a drive through the Hills.

I saw the landscape as he loved it.
We stopped at Spearfish Canyon
and Bridal Veil Falls to enjoy
the autumn color changes.
He drove us past Crazy Horse
where we remarked the carving
was perpetually in progress.

Six years later, we buried our
mother in the family cemetery
next to Dad. I listened to Jim
educate his sons about crystal
formations unique to the Hills.

I showed my husband
the Needle's Eye and took home
a photograph to remind me.
I felt dwarfed by the granite spires
and inspired by the vast vistas
which overlooked the hills and valleys.

When Jim died, I looked again
at my Black Hills photograph
of the sun radiated over the top,
threaded through the crack,
and imagined Jim's spirit traveled
through that Needle's Eye.

Written in 2011

Thrown Off

Chug, chug, chug.
I drank the gallon.
My stomach churned.
I felt woozy and sloshed
when I walked up the sloping floor
to the dart board,
teetered on tiptoes,
and pulled out the darts.

I tested the points
and licked blood drops
from my fingertips.
Whoosh, whoosh,
my blue-feathered friends
both stuck in the bull's eye.
I'd promised him, I'd get better
if I could just drink all my water.
Now I gotta go pee an ocean
before I can high-five my partner.

Written Aug 2012 from a (super human) prompt at PST-NE

Time

a Minute form

We can set clock
ticks to our time,
          choose the seasons
today, whether
fall back again
          to Spring reasons.

We think we can
decide each rhyme,
          order the space,
set careful plans.
Time ticks today,
          controls our pace.

Written in 2009

Time Passes

Time stacked another grain,
one grit of sand,
wheelchair slow in youth,
mid-life mosquito fast.
The nows and thens
heralded ancient thunder.

Written in 2008

To a Rescued Spitz

He returned you to the pound,
because you bit me twice.
I'm sorry, Missy.
No one learned,
we only argued over
a dropped orange peel.

Written in 2010 from prompt in Karen Golightly class
in Memphis, Tennessee

To My Ex

He was the one I loved.
We enjoyed life together.
I cared about him.
Strong, but unsure of himself,
he was the one I worried about.
I was his. I thought he was mine.
He disagreed. I understood.
Once I loved him.

Written in 1995

Tobacco Barn

A brave weathered tobacco barn
sits sentry on a hill, ignores
urbanity sprawl invasion into
diminished open farmland.

Untrimmed forsythia bushes
wave in each direction
at close threats from
construction trucks.

A lonely rural railroad town
now fights expected
neighboring city absorption,
resists loss of identity.

Weathered boards crack
in disrepair against progress.
The tobacco barn stands
as unnecessary as a cigarette.

Posted online on Poetic Asides *2009*

To My Perfect Friend or Partner

To my perfect friend or partner:
Are we on parallel paths?
Do we move in the same direction,
but not in the same place or time?

Will we converge one day?
Have we already met and
didn't recognize each other?
Or were our past lives
together too traumatic?

Once our longing is satisfied
in this life, will we look forward
to another one? Will we watch for,
or avoid, each other again?

Written in 2010 in NeSCC Creative Writing class

To Your Health

Sparkling water,
second only
to unpolluted air.
The more I drink,
the more I think,
water must be
nothing but pure.

Written in 2009

Tonight is the Night

for Scott and Kim Anderson, at their Aruba wedding celebration
August 16, 2008

Tonight is the night you've chosen to wed.
You speak, *I love you.* Promises are said.

You exchanged faithful vows of truth and trust.
Years will pass. Don't let oaths gather dust.

Enjoy this moment with family and friends.
Beach swept clean for red carpet altar ends.

Formal attire without a white glove.
Reality far away. Tonight your love.

Now have fun, party, enjoy this time, play.
You should state, *I love you* every day.

It might be enough to hold each other
against the world. Celebrate, don't smother.

You speak, *I love you.* Promises are said.
Tonight is the night you've chosen to wed.

Written in 2008

Tornado

a Haiku form

Tornado warning,
a swirling, fear-inducing
genuine alarm.

1977 Written for DWU Creative Writing

Tourist Season

Black Hills, South Dakota

attractions open,
gas prices soar,
higher restaurant rates,
clever artifact artists,
no vacancies.
Here come the tourists.

crazy traffic,
ignored street signs,
poor lost souls,
messy picnic areas,
littered campgrounds,
wildlife hiding,

fill your cash register,
pretend your wagon train was massacred,
give stupid answers to ignorant questions,
move away for the season,
or look happy and content.
Here come the tourists.

Written in 1987; 2012 published in Fall Edition of
Pasque Petals, the *SDSPS anthology*

Train and Retrain

I face forward on
the train; I'll get
there before you do.

But, face backwards
you'll see where
we've been.

Written in 2004

Train Thoughts

Eyes close,
head bobs
with the rhythm
of the wheels.

Written in 2004

Tribute to Forest Firemen

He fights the fire courageously
with steel shovel and heavy hose,
inhales smoke and smoldered cinders.

Deer and rabbit run ahead, leap
fallen trees, trample dry leaves.
Flames laugh, push animals from home.

Concerned fireman fights
crimson landscapes, prevents
forest from reduction to ashes.

Wind giggles, fans sparks
onto fresh dry fuel, makes containment
stay just out of his frustrated reach.

Prayers at last reach the Rainmaker,
who calms the wind and settles the issue.
Trees sizzle and smoke hisses.

Weary arms fight on, stand guard,
keep fires from re-ignition,
avoid spread, and irreparable damages.

Finally, he can rest, bathe, eat without
smoke-coughs, and sleep peacefully.
He knows the blazes are finally out.

Courage and skill saved the majority
of the park and our beautiful forests.
Grateful applause rarely reaches weary ears.

Written in 1988, Published in Tennessee Voices
Anthology 2008-09

Triple Delight Treat

The triple chocolate fudge,
filled with macadamia nuts,
smelled sooo loud, I became
deaf, but inhaled its perfume.

Insatiable taste buds
arrested my willpower,
demanded one nibble,
a teensy bite, and then
I devoured the evidence.

Calories consumed
in private, overflowed
my favorite blue jeans.
I wiggled and jumped,
but they would not zip.

Thank you, elastic waistband,
my forever best friend.
You stretch and stretch
to let me breathe and bend.

Written in 2009,
published in Tennessee Voices Anthology 2010-11,
2010 last stanza in Lost State Voices, Vol. III,
and 2011 in PST-NE's Funny you should say that. . .

Triverse

a Triverse form

Try a verse,
a triverse,
on for size.

      Does it fit your poem
      and are you satisfied
      that three's a nice number?

Triple sentences,
tri-stanzas,
three is just right.

1977 Written for DWU Creative Writing class

Trouble

Tumultuous emotions
steer my life.
I'm in trouble
and can't escape.
My love's in trouble,
so is my life.

1977 Written for DWU Creative Writing class

Truck Driver Blues

I'll think of your kiss.
        You I'll miss.
I'll miss your touch,
        so very much.
I'll remember this day.
        Please, please stay.
I'll miss your smile
        a little while.
I'll miss your nose?
        So, who knows.
I love you, Chuck
        with a bit o'luck

your truck may pay
        some day.
Yes, we might, hey,
        we may,
before I'm buried,
        be married.
How happy we'll be,
        just you and me.

Written in 1970

Truly Peaceful

A beta bowl was a new invention for me.
I was fascinated when I first noticed one.
The lady said, "Buy a peace lily and a beta fish."

Beta fish, a fierce attitude, facing his own reflection.
Peace lilies survive in water without dirt.
A warring fish and a peaceful plant combined.

The fish, I named Truly, was a brilliant true blue
Peaceful was already written on the lily's tag.
Quietly, I watched Truly feed from the roots of Peaceful.

I was sad to find Truly dead, floating on top the water.
The turquoise crystal pebbles shined in the vase bottom.
The peace lily refused to bloom, wilted, never recovered.

The day before 9/11 was the last day,
I lived with Truly Peaceful.

Written in 2001

Trusting

Teenager Tommy asked his grandfather,
"How can someone you cannot see
be the one you trust?"

The old man answered with a sigh,
"All I know is that I must.
I cannot see you as clearly now,

and yet I've been asked to adjust.
It's hard to explain, but not difficult to believe.
I may not see my Lord, but I feel Him."

"Feel Him? As easily as I touch you now?"

"Yes, as easily.
I feel Him in my soul.
I feel Him when I'm happy.
When I'm sad, He is here.
I trust my cares to Him,
when I'm worried or I'm mad.

A tactile belief I feel
with more than my fingers.
I will feel Him when I'm dust.
He is my Lord, and He will be just.
Therefore, my son,
I believe I cannot help but trust."

2003 published in The Way of the Cross

Tsunami

I.

a Haiku form

Earth quakes,
mountainous wave,
coast line reclaimed.

Written in 2005

Tsunami

II.

Epic eras of tides splashed
coastlines for millennia,
added and subtracted.
Nature remains control mistress.

Real estate brokers believe
valuables belong near
unpredictable water.
Wake up calls are harsh.

Written in 2009

Turning Point

Kit, with other gutter chicks,
flocked nightly to the Buck 'N Gator.
The owners of the wannabe bar,
wanted to be world travelers.

The customers, who came on Harleys or
Hondas, with honeys, were laborers,
PTSD* vets, and the unemployed.
They wanted to shoot whiskey and beer.

She wanted to be someone else,
carry on meaningless conversations,
and drink a Tom Collins,
or two, or more.

When ignored, she called
the bartender ugly and
threw a glass. Refused
her favorite anesthetic,

she tried another path.
Kit found who she didn't
want to be when
she was eighty-sixed.

*Post-traumatic stress disorder

Written in 1989

Two Drifting Boats

The waves tease us,
push you against me.
We bump and giggle.
I nudge your back.
We bob in the surf.

I, sky-striped;
you, sunshiny bright.
We are not quite twins
moored within a sea
by an elevated dock.

You motored away, tickled
the surface and left wake,
careless of return maps.
Gray water scrapes my belly.
Seagulls perch on my bow.

Tethered, I wait for you,
understand the widow's walk.
I can't touch your side.
I bob and list, twist,
swirl, pull my ropes.

I'm freed to roam the seas,
the oceans, and across horizons.
Determined to find my loss,
I search the salty vastness
and question. Were you ever mine?

Written in 2009

Two Rivers in One

an Economic Flood

I.

Shimmer, flow, ripple,
tumble over barbed rocks.
Float the recession away.
Listen to bird conversations,
wonder who we think we are.
Photograph perfect serenity
before raindrops shoo us home.

II.

Bank overflows expectations.
Drop after drop deepens concern.
Mud piles up. Tree limbs push debris,
congest rapids, and water surges.
Wildlife flies or runs for shelter.
Humans don't learn to move homes
away from water's unpredictability.

2009 Honorable Mention PST Annual Mid-south Poetry Festival

Under Construction

Oh, the smell of fresh tar –
the pungent odor
makes me nauseous.

One-lane traffic,
hot weather,
hotter tempers.

Workers stand around
with hands in pockets,
drive back and forth,
tie up traffic,

wave slow and stop signs.
How slow must we crawl?
Oh, the joys of the
construction season.

Written in 2004

Understanding

I don't understand you.
       Maybe we all think of ourselves.
You believe you are better than anyone else.

You are continually trying to prove it,
       when you know you don't have to for me.

I'm very confused.
       I'm afraid of this world.
              I'm afraid to live, to die.

Are you afraid and confused, too?
       Now, I understand.

Written in 1968

Unisex Souls

Souls are neither
male nor female.
They are not definitely
one or the other.
There are no genders
in the hereafter.

Written in 2004

Universe Shift

The day you died, Jim,
I became the elder,
the last of the four Roses.
Soon I will outlive your years,
and be older than you.

Written in 2009

Ups and Downs

Eightieth Floor:
Homeless? No, not you –
ten-thousand-dollar
island wedding, new cars,
designer clothes.

Fiftieth Floor:
lower pay, fewer hours,
less in, more out,
scarce jobs. . .
Foreclosure!

Tenth Floor:
temporary or part-time. . .
not good enough?
Sit in your recliner
with grumbling stomach.

Second Floor:
Unemployment benefits
don't last forever
nor family hospitality.
Is this working for you?

Ground Floor:
The good life elevator
zoomed to the top.
A beautiful view you
borrowed on bad credit.

Basement:
Nowhere but up.
Don't panic! Start over.
Take deep breaths.
Climb the stairs next time.

2010 3ʳᵈ Place March PST monthly contest

Van Pool

Fort Meade, South Dakota

Although I haven't been long
a passenger of the famous van pool,
I'd like to share my impressions
none of which are cruel.

Everyone is pleasant but mostly
Just sleepy. No one's been snoring,
except silly me during a nap
when our commute was boring.

Dean has been our bus driver.
He never says step to the rear,
looks his list over and checks twice
before putting our van in gear.

Always he's been ready to smile,
though the sun just finished dawning.
We grunt at him and find a seat,
to his pleasant good morning.

We sleep, joke, gossip, or
complain endlessly about work.
We have several professions
including at least one clerk.

Thirteen passenger seats,
not all are daily filled.
If there's someone who wants
to ride with us, they'd gladly be billed.

Once in a while on Fridays
we pull into Mickey D's for coffee
or juice. Sometimes there are donuts
and even pizza which surprised me.

Lively conversations, I heard
when we were trying to decide
where to celebrate an event.
Many good choices were denied.

So enjoy your dinner,
Lola, Carol, Rich, Larry.
I'm no longer a passenger,
Ruth, Lois and Woody.

Written in 1985

Vertically Challenged

short and wide,
but, oh, so sweet

queen-size full-measure,
outstretched reach
grasps life's liberal share

wide horizontal smile,
drips sweet volumes
of pungent perfume

expansive, vast
with ample range,
not tall and stately

extensive, compact,
not immense,
chunky, stout, broad

and smells,
oh, so, good.

2005 Published in Schrom Hills Park *chapbook*

Violin Practice

That fateful high school day my mother's violin
made magical music for me. The conductor
announced I'd won the challenge from the last chair
of the second violins. Mom reacted like I'd played
in the Philharmonic. I wasn't surprised at her next plan.

Me? Challenge the next chair and move up? I groaned,
because I couldn't tune it without breaking strings.
The orchestra leader just tells me to hand it to him.
I run to my room, recall I'd begged to quit every year.

Mother remembered when she and her sister enjoyed
playing concerts. She choose a piece for me to practice.
She just knew I would like orchestra.
"Mom, we're not the same. I don't care about violin

and I'm not playing that thing anymore."
I wanted to play our old black upright piano with
yellowed sticky keys, far better than Mom's
squawky violin.

She says they can't afford piano lessons.
I'm surprised she wanted to play piano, too.
Mom nodded. "You stick it out this year, and
I'll discuss it with your father next year."

It wasn't over, but I stared at Mom, imagined her
in high school. She wanted something
she couldn't have. Mother smiled.
Maybe we're not so different after all.

*2004 Written in Rose Solari's Poem-A-Day class
at the Writers' Center*

Virginal Snow

That first snow
outlined the park bench,
snowflakes piled up,
fell among the slats,
caressed its shape,
like a cruel first love.

Written in 2005

Virginity Unlocked

Virginity had become
a broken padlock.
All that was secure and safe
had become open.

Written in 2004

Visitor

. . . and if I call
he will be my brother again
remind me I'm the little sister.
I'll need to admit I love him
even when he knows it all,
all his right answers.
He'll expect to find my weaknesses
and pour ice water into my cracks.

I'll ask where he is unloading
his semi-tractor trailer this day
I never know his time zone
or when it's okay to call
during his evening minutes.

I need to report
on our mother's decline.
I wait for him to answer,
and dread his turn my way.

2009 Written in SCWW poetry workshop with Anne Barnhill

W

Waiting

a *Tanka form*

Waiting is wasteful,
nerve-racking, irritating.
He would like to scream.
While he's patiently waiting,
I am always late.

1977 Written for DWU Creative Writing class

Wake Up

Morning?
>   Already?
>>   This day has begun.

Sleepy eyes open.
>>   Look at the sunshine.

Yawn!
>   It's cloudy?
>>   I'm going back to bed.

1977 Written for DWU Creative Writing class

War is Dirty

War is dirty:
filthy bombs,
grimy bullets,
muddy trenches,
soiled soldiers,
grungy wounds,
littered lives,
trashed towns,
sooty streets,
murky policies,
broken promises,
dusty patriotism.
Please clean up
peace talks and
rebuild those
tortured lives.

Posted on Poetic Asides *2009*

Warning Signs

a Pirouette form

Crossed double yellow lines,
she disregarded friendship
and the stop signs of
churched marital pacts
the husband abandoned.

The husband abandoned
her for his loving wife.
Children played unaware
this U-turn kept him from
divorce and child support.

2010 3ʳᵈ Place PST Annual Mid-South Poetry Festival

Waterfall Ballet

Perfect paradise, turquoise pool,
waterfall shower, dancing swans,
filtered sunlight, tropical plants,
sultry water combs my hair,
kisses my face, flows over my trunk.
Plumeria fragrance fills my nostrils.
Cares ripple, fish whisper.
Faint music stretches . . .
     "Mom, Mom." What? An earthquake shakes me.
I pirouette in slow motion.
Clement water massages,
nourishes my bottom.
On pointe, I kiss the cascade.
Massage arms first, then toes,
legs and everywhere,
round my shoulders.
Now cup my breasts . . .
     "MOM MOM MOM"   What...who...where...?
     "Sissie's in the bathroom." "Okay, okay."
     "Mommy I got to . . ."   "Now?"
     "Yes, Mommie, NOW!!"   "Just this time,
         Nickie, promise you won't let neighbors
         see you pee in the yard!"

Close my eyes. Return
to paradise. Waterfall,
consume me. Drift away
to Saturday morning's dream.
     KNOCK, KNOCK, KNOCK
         Angry neighbor's voice says,
         "Nickie's watered my azalea again."

Written in 2005

Water Lilies

Painted by Claude Monet
an Ekphrastic form

Tadpole green dominated
buttered pots of lily plates,
smeared with dabs of bloody promises,
leaked periwinkle streaked the sand
gobbled underwater for recycling.

2009 Written at Abingdon, Virginia Creative Writing Day
with Carolyn Kreiter-Foronda, Poet Laureate of Virginia

Way Back When

While the beautician shampooed my hair,
I heard a customer ask,
"Wasn't gas a buck eighty a gallon then?"
That sounded like a long time ago.

In my brain's file cabinet I explored
a folder labeled nineteen-sixty-nine, when
two-hundred-ninety-five dollars bought
my first car, a nine-year-old Ford Fairlane.

Faded Blue and I learned to drive together.
We cruised Eighth Street until curfew
or explored the Black Hills on our own.
For once, I didn't need to hitch a ride.

On Interstate 90 the tires shimmied
at eighty miles per hour. In the fast lane
the steering wheel shook at ninety,
the scenery blurred at one-hundred.

We did it! We felt alive! My heart raced,
but I swallowed hard. I looked for cops,
feared accidents. I slowed us down to sixty.
We'd passed Ellsworth and arrived in Wall.

After I explored the famous drug store,
patted the stuffed jackalope, indulged myself
with a buffalo burger, and ice cream cone,
I drove a slower fifty miles back to Rapid City.

Written in 2011

Weather Beater

Handwritten For Sale signs,
dotted Florida's hurricane beaten coast.
Billboards exclaim no Low Country
in one part of South Carolina.

We spent one night without
electricity, listened to storms
and threats of lightning.

Weather, weather everywhere
and not a safe place to live.

Written in 2010

Wedding Song for Mother and Son

You are not my little boy any more.
I can't take you in my arms.
Save you from the monkey bars.
Now you tower above me.

Kiss me just once more.
Take her in your arms.
She'll save you being lonely.
Now blend your lives together.

Written in 2008

Weed

I saw a weed today,
perfectly shaped.
The wind made it
quake and loose its seeds.

Weeds don't need love,
just dirt, sunshine, rain,
and a place to die quietly
where no mourner will cry.

If weeds could
experience love,
would they multiply
and live much longer?

Written in 2004

Weeding

The wind quaked
a mature dandelion
and released seeds
from a silk snowflake.

The gardener shuddered
at invasion of planned order.

Weeds request no love,
just dirt, sunshine, rain,
a place to put down roots,
and die with dry eyes.

Imagine, if weeds were nurtured,
they would require no weeding.

Written in 2011

Weeping Tree

Spring green weeps
from the tree.
Will this barn
last as long as me?

Will all be gone –
all green spaces –
under an ultra-marathon
of bulldozer interfaces?

Cry, farmland, and pray
that your landscape
won't erode every day
into a streetscape.

2008 published in Barn Charm *chapbook*

Welcome

All I could see was blackness.
My hand stretched out, groped.
Stretched further, there was only empty space.
I shuffled one step at a time . . . slowly. . . slowly.

I touched the rough wall where the wallpaper
ended and the doorway began.
The blackness surrounded me again.
Oh! I stubbed my toe on the footstool.

I winced until the pain stopped. I shivered.
Cold milk dribbled on my hand.
In a few steps I would reach the railing.
I walked up the stairs, then down the hall.

I scanned for anything in my way.
The bedroom door was closed.
I reached for the light.
How terrible to always be blind like that.

Written in 1968

Well-Crafted

an Etheree form

I
must reach
way up high,
past shoddy work,
climb a steep ladder,
dream my future, live proud,
create my hoped perfection.
Not my intent to float *en masse*
But stretch and achieve to realize:
Miters make square corners when craft matters.

Written in 2010,
2012 Honorable mention from Grandmother Earth/Life Press
Christian Writers Awards for short forms,
Published in Grandmother Earth Volume XI

What a Pill!

Doctors! You make me angry.
You think you're God's gift
to sick people. What do you
really know about WELLNESS?

Sickness is your specialty.
People suffer to pay for your
Lexus, your Tudor mansion,
and your kids' ivy league tuition.

One pill treats one symptom,
another six pills alleviate
side effects and so forth and
so on to employ more researchers.

Did you take nutrition classes?
Will you recommend, "An apple
a day to keep the doctor away."?
Or would that hurt your practice?

Don't bow down to pharmaceuticals.
Don't look for a magic pill.
Embrace natural food sources.
Synthetic vitamins don't count.

Tell patients, to stop serving
high fructose and don't gobble
saturated fat. Encourage healthy
eating to make it socially acceptable.

Prevention is still the best
invention for wellness.

Posted on Poetic Asides *2009*

Pastiche of Poetry

What for?

What are
curtains for,
but to hide behind
and peek-a-boo?
What are cribs
but cages
for playing children?

Written in 1973

What Good is War?

War makes enemies.
    Enemies kill, make more enemies.
        Killing enemies makes more enemies.
What good is war?

Peace makes allies.
    Allies prosper, make more allies.
        Loving allies makes more allies.
Peace is what is good.

Written in 2004

What if . . .

What if . . .
you loved me
>   and you gave me exclusive rights,
>   and you missed me when we were apart,
>   and you called me almost every day,
>   and you sent flowers and a balloon bouquet,
>   and you depended on me,
>   and you leaned on me,
>   and you confided in me,
AND What if I loved you?

Written in 1989

What I'm About

I'm about: traveled to all fifty states
looked for life, survived Charm City
and Capitol Hill, and settled in the clear blue skies
of southern Appalachia with my electrician
who constantly attempts to ground my spirit.
I planted roses once again. They root.
I tend to move on. Maybe we'll stay put
to allow me to take root, blossom,
and endure milder four seasons,
while I write until I have nothing more to say.

Written in 2008

What is Love?

'Tis naught, but a lover's dream.
Things are different so it'll seem.
Let me look in your eyes. Look in mine.
Your eyes will sparkle. Mine will shine.
Today the dark seems so light.
The wrong now appears so right.

Written in 1990

What is the Measure of God?

How many cubits tall is God?
He must be higher than the loftiest mountain
and vaster than outer space.

How many talents does He weigh?
He could be as light as a feather of Spring air
or He weighs heavy on a mourning heart.

How old is God?
He's as young as a newborn smile and trillions of years
into forever. He remembers our first and last days.

How close is God?
He's as far as the stars and
yet only a handbreadth away.

What color is God?
He's a crystal prism reflecting rainbow colors,
but so transparent we can't claim He's from any race.

How much is God worth?
He's measured in love, not coins or precious stones.
God is free to everyone, but precious for too few.

Whew! I think that God must be
immeasurable, timeless, and priceless.
God is beyond reason and enveloped in our souls.

2003 Published in The Way of the Cross,
2005 in Faith and Spirit *chapbook,*
and 2010 in Spiritual Reflections by PST-NE

What's Left?

Where has the sky gone?
God's beautiful blue sky.
It's disappeared, gone.
It's gray and ugly.
I can't see the sun any more.

Where has the air gone?
God's clear fresh air
has disappeared, gone.
It's thick and smoky.
I can't deep breathe.

Where has the grass gone?
God's green Spring grass
has disappeared, gone.
It's full of glass and tin cans.
I can't walk barefoot here.

Where has love gone?
God's marvellous unique love
has disappeared, gone.
The world's full of hate and prejudice.
No one speaks kind words.

Where has the water gone?
God's clear sparkling water
has disappeared, gone.
It's full of waste and chemicals.
I thirst for purity ever more.

Where has God gone?
Our all seeing, all doing God.
No, don't take away my hope.
I can live, if I still believe in something.
Take Him and nothing is left.

Written in 2004

When Mother was Done

I wish I could have foreseen
all the unanswered questions.
Do you remember when we. . .?
What's so and so's name?
Why didn't you tell me
it was your last day?

Once, you said you'd done
all you wanted to do and
looked forward to nothing.
Were you really finished?
I fear I buried your secret
unfulfilled thoughts and dreams.

Posted on Poetic Asides *2009*

Who are We?

Green masks
cover our color.
Mechanical voices
disguise our accents.
Tented cloaks
hide our gender.
Age not detected.

We're not vanilla,
chocolate or strawberry.
Neapolitan stirred to mud.
Personality is nothing.
Upbringing camouflaged.
Relationships sidelined.
Education inconsequential.

Who are we?
Are we our ethnic race,
our gender, our station?
If all is covered, our
souls must find an outlet,
or be lost forever
as no one special.

Written in 2009

Who Gets Him Then?

Baby is cuddled and
played with until he cries.
Then who gets him?

Baby is talked to and exclaimed over
until he becomes damp.
Then who gets him?

Baby is cute when he dumps
his bowl of cereal on his head.
Then who gets him?

Baby gets sympathy
when he gets a cold or flu.
Who gets sick next?

Mother, of course!

Written in 1972 shortly after Erik, my second son, was born

Who was I?

Petals scattered, thorns no longer prick me.
I've been called several names.
That's me, a mixture of who I am and
who I once was. I will always be a Rose.

My ashes will no longer blossom, but sit
in a small dark box buried with
my husband, my ancestors, my cousins.

My headstone may say,
"Life was a research project;
I'm ready for my final grade."

Maybe my spirit will float
in a hot air balloon
above Lancaster, Pennsylvania.
Hopefully, I will be at peace.

Written in 2012 in Jesse Graves workshop sponsored by PST-NE

Wild Acres

Quiet rustic retreat
      for introspective reflection,
rain-silenced katydids,
      laughing friends,
pensive moments,
      mountain solitude.

Written in 2008

Wild and Free

I am free and wild like
an untrimmed forsythia bush,
rooted by a decayed barn.
I stretch for the sky,
gesture at construction trucks,
which labor to neighborhood plats.
I hate those new signs of civilization.

2008 Published in Barn Charm *chapbook*

Wind and Snow

a Haiku form

Hushed wind stops swirling.
Drifted winter bed whispers.
Freed snow-angel dreams.

Published on FanStory.com *2008*

Winter

a Tanka form

Clouds translucently
clutter the wintertime sky.
Iced meringue snow grieves.
Frosting dissolves to gray mush.
Sun warms frigid attitudes.

1977 Written for Creative Writing class at DWU,
2008 earned Honorable Mention in
PST Annual Mid-South Poetry Festival

Winter Walk

Shivering, we trudge
our snow whispered park.
Snowflakes stopped,
settled their free fall
on a favorite park bench.
Melded perfect layers
outline uninviting planks,
a respite for warmer days.
Now, we follow yesterday's
footprints of loving togetherness
and later find a cozier place
to warm each other again.

2005 published in Schrom Hills Park *chapbook and* *2011* Images of Love *Anthology by PST-NE*

Wipe Your Tears

Wipe your tears, wipe your tears away.
Put a smile, put a smile back on,
for the next moment will be better.
It can't be as bad as you say.

Sing a song, sing a song again.
Let your blues, let your blues go away.
For the moment we'll be happy.
It could just be you will now win.

Written in 1989

Without Me in this World

Without me existing in this world:

My dad would not have had a daughter to hold
his hand and read the 23rd Psalm on his last day.

My mother would not have moved to Tennessee
We would not have reacquainted ourselves.

Jim would not have been jealous of his little sister.
He might have lived with less irritation in his world.

Erik would not have been born only
to die early from my carelessness.

Rob would not have listened to me
about retiring early to enjoy golf and hiking.

Scott would not celebrate another year.
        His birth is the most important event,
        I accomplished in this life.

Posted on Poetic Asides *2011*

Woman – Bitch

Woman
cooperative, nice,
but stand up for rights?
Bitch!

1977 Written for DWU Creative Writing class

Womb

I floated,
enjoyed
floating,
floating
eternally.

Late arrival
funnel cloud
sucked and
swirled me
in Mom's womb.

Doctor hears
twin hearts beat.
Mother gasps.
Him and me?
Crowded, confused.

His soul
undecided.
Stay? Go?
I nudged him out.

I stay.
Only one baby.
Daddy cries,
Whew!

Written in 2008

Woodland Ballet

Dancing leaves
sway in the breeze
to mockingbird melodies.

Balon perfected
arch, reach,
swing, fling.

Wait, wish
wonder,
when muddy toes
will be freed for *on pointe*
ready for *arabesque* and *adagio*.

2005 published in Schrom Hills Park *chapbook*

Word Diet

Lately, I've dieted on words:
sweet, sour,
salty, crispy, crunchy.

Some I've chewed on.
Others have been
hard to swallow.

Written in 2002

Words

Non-communication is worse than quarrels.
Not speaking, not listening, leads to doubt.

Along with that doubt comes fear.
Memory is a tortured evil thing.

It tries to twist your thoughts.
Blot my mind or give me words.

Let me not turn on friends,
because words were not said.

With words, you can forgive or forget.
Let them understand: words are important.

Written in 1965

Work

Boredom
tedious, tiresome,
yawn, sleepy, drone

1977 Written for DWU Creative Writing class

Work Again

Work
difficult challenge
figure, file, type
make the numbers agree
Bookkeeping

1977 Written for DWU Creative Writing class

World Stage

All the World's a Stage and all the men and women merely players.
William Shakespeare

The world's stage is now
truly global with economic
and energetic impact.

A shot heard 'round
the world* is not as loud
as a silent cash register.

No longer self-contained,
one human life's baby steps:
tickle time, affect millions.

Dependency on foreign
commodities produces
more carbon footprints.

Seemingly tiny litter
is not easily erased
before ruining the planet.

Shipments bound
for anywhere poison
babies, dogs, and more.

Earth is outbalanced
with technology.
Gray became the new green.

Smog-filled skies,
carbon emitted from
vehicles, pesticides.

Warnings fall on
blue-toothed ears
littering air waves.

Wake up, World.
It's your stage.
Play the protagonist roles.

Concord Hymn by Ralph Waldo Emerson

2009 3ʳᵈ Place PST May Monthly Contest

Worm Spit at Watauga Lake

Last summer
we squished
wiggly worms
onto our hooks.

I said,
"No point
to talk politics."

You replied,
"Sure, such words
only get all mushy
when the fish
spit on the line."

2009 Written from a prompt at SCWW
led by Anne Barnhill

Worth the Trouble

a Jaleen form

Prune, trim and groom, I pick
bugs from dead leaves
and off my sleeves.
Perfect flowers I greet.

Roses bloom, soothe the sick,
peach, yellow, red.
Petals outgrew weeds,
which thrived at their feet.

Written in 2009

Xmas

a Haiku form

Christmas has become
just a four-letter word of
commercialism.

Written in 1987

Yellowstone Park Bison

While we snowmobiled
Yellowstone's snow-packed
highway, I pointed at bison,
older than time. They foraged grass,

rocked their massive heads
in leaden rhythm against fallen snow.
Slower and lower they pushed piles
right and left to find sufficient food.

Massive bison herds once ranged,
hunters slaughtered for food and furs.
Occasionally, mystics glimpsed
one snow-camouflaged sentinel.

We cruised farther, but
reluctantly yielded to a herd
which blocked our rutted road.
We eyed them. They glared at us.

Helmeted and snowsuit zipped,
without glass windows to roll up,
I felt naked against huge beasts.
My heart pounded. Time erased time.

Perhaps they thought us odd,
to leave our zigzag tracks.
After a shake of bulky heads,
they lumbered across our path.

White clouds of long-held
breath escaped my mouth as
our noisy engines roared away
from their last claimed territory.

Written in 1984

You are Deep in my Heart

You are
deep in my heart.
Please know,
I know
your pain.

Written in 1985

You Call that a Sneeze?

It was just a tiff.
I have louder hiccups.
Mine are attic clearing
forces from the gut
at hurricane force.

They don't foreshadow
or predict diseases
but just plain clear my air.

My sneeze-jags often
produce twelve in a row.
My husband tires
of *God Blessing* me.

Maybe I just need
heavy duty prayer.
So I'll let 'er rip.

Written in 2009

You Eat too Fast

to the Simon and Garfunkel's 59th Street Bridge song Feeling Groovy

Slow down.
You eat too fast.
You got to make
the cookies last.
Just swilling down
some soda pop
and feeling guilty.

Written in 2012

You Surround Me

I looked skyward
to find connection with God.

You, Holy Spirit, are my
extension cord.
Your energies surround me,
electrify the air I breathe.

God is not far away
from His agents.

They smile, hug,
guide, protect me
from myself and life's
unexpected crashes.

Written in 2012

Z

ZZZ

I have to finish this
so I'll have time for that.
I have to finish that,
then I'll have extra time.
I've finished at last.
Now, I have time to
Zzzzzzzzzzzzzzz Zzzzzzzzzzzzzzzz Zzzzzzzzzzzzzzz
Zzzzzzzzzzzzzzz Zzzzzzzzzzzzzzzz Zzzzzzzzzzzzzzz

1977 Written for DWU Creative Writing

No, no, no! Wait!

Don't go to sleep yet.
Turn the page.
Acknowledgements follow.
I have many more people to thank.

Send me your favorite poem.
Connect on my website at
http://www.RoseKlix.com

ACKNOWLEDGEMENTS

I apologize up front for the length of this section. However, it took more than one village to raise this poet. I've been well-blessed with poetry lovers in my world. I seem to find them no matter where I live.

Educators: Thank you to the following Creative Writing instructors who enhanced my poetry craft. I could not have written for this collection without the knowledge I received from **Mrs. Speakman** my fifth-grade teacher at Lincoln Grade School and **Myrna Haight** at Rapid City High School, **Dr Mary S. Weinkauf** my English major advisor and creative writing professor at Dakota Wesleyan University (DWU) in Mitchell, South Dakota (Thanks for your assignment to write sixty poems that semester), and **Gretchen McCroskey** a recent creative writing instructor for a refresher course at Northeast State Community College (NeSCC) in Blountville, TN.

More Poet Teachers: I attended several readings and workshops led by established poets: National Poet Laureate **Ted Kooser** at the Library of Congress (I love the Valentines you sent me!); **Dr. Michael S. Glaser**, Poet Laureate of Maryland; (Our Greenbelt Writers' Showcase key-note speaker**); Dr. Carolyn Kreiter-Foronda**, (Virginia's Poet Laureate, who taught me more about ekphrastic poetry); **Cathy Smith Bowers**, North Carolina Poet Laureate, (who introduced me to the ghazal form); **Anne Waldman** at my first workshop, sponsored by Black Hills Writers Group (BHWG); **Bill Brown, Jane Hicks** the *Cosmic Possum*, (Your prompts inspire emotional memories); Anne Barnhill and Anne Hicks (both at South Carolina Writers Workshops (SCWW), Myrtle Beach; **Dr. Jesse Graves** at ETSU (Sorry I don't write as a southerner.); **Elizabeth Hunter** (Thank you for also encouraging me to write creative nonfiction) at the Buffalo Mountain Writers Workshop (ETSU); and the many talented poets at Writers Center at Bethesda, Maryland, especially: **Elizabeth Rees**, **Laura Fargas** (Sorry my "Beowulf" reading sickened you), and **Rose Solari** in the challenging Poem-A-Day class (Thank you for trying to teach me to write less prose-like).

Thank you to the following organizations, peers, mentors, judges and editors for acknowledging my poetry in their workshops, contests and/or publications. When available, I provide their website addresses.

IN SOUTH DAKOTA

- South Dakota State Poetry Society (SDSPS), especially **Rosemary Moeller** Thank you for trusting me to judge the chapbook contest titled Four Quarters to a Section. www.sdstatepoetrysociety.com
- Colleges of Mid-America editors, *CMA Review,* a consortium of Midwest colleges

Rapid City:

- Black Hills Writers Group (BHWG), especially founder **Laura Bowers Van Nuys** http://blackhillswritersgroup.org/
- Black Hills chapter of the National League of American Penwomen, especially **Irene Kverne** http://www.nlapw.org/nlapw-branches/
- Central States Fair judges

Mitchell:

- Dakota Wesleyan University editors of *Prairie Winds*

Huron:

- South Dakota State Fair judges, Huron

Vermillion:

- South Dakota Literary Project editors, *Dakota: Plains & Fancy*

IN MARYLAND

Bethesda

- Writers' Center, I enjoyed attending a variety of workshops led by MFA graduates http://www.writer.org/

Greenbelt

- *Greenbelt News*, weekly newspaper Vol 67 No.31 (Thank you for breaking your "no poetry" rule!)
- Greenbelt Writers Group, especially **Carol Griffith** and *The Sound of Words*, Oral Anthology producers, http://www.oocities.org/thegwg/
- Holy Cross Lutheran Church, *The Way of the Cross*, (It was fun being the Poet in Residence, when the secretary challenged me to write a poem for each newsletter.)
- *Iguana Review* editor **Rob Baluch**, Greenbelt

- Saturday Greenbelt Library gatherings where **Jim Link** knew all the dirt on famous poets
- My chapbooks: *Faith and Spirit* and *Schrom Hills Park*

Millersville
- Christ Lutheran Church, *The Messenger* newsletter

IN TENNESSEE

Tri-Cities (Johnson City, Bristol, TN & VA, and Kingsport):
- Lost State Writers Guild, *Lost State Voices,* especially **Carol Jackson** and **Sylvia Nichels** http://loststatewritersguild.com/

Blountville:
- Northeast State Community College (NeSCC), *Echoes and Images* anthology 2011 editors especially **Tamara Baxter**, and **Gretchen McCroskey**, http://www.northeaststate.edu/
- Poetry Society of Tennessee – Northeast branch (PST-NE), http://pstne. weebly.com/ (Anthologies: *Spiritual Reflections* edited **by Marlene Simpson** and **John Summers**, *Images of Love* edited by **Ben Dugger** and **John Jenkins**, and *Funny You Should Say That* edited by **Todd Bailey**

Cordova
- *Grandmother Earth*, especially editor **Frances Cowden** http://grand-motherearth.org/

Elizabethton:
- Watauga branch of the National League of American Penwomen, especially my sponsor **Martha S. Culp,** President **Judy Donley**, and Secretary **Martha Query**, http://www.nlapw.org/

Gray:
- My 2008 chapbook: *Barn Charm*
- Washington County Library for sponsoring my "Adventures in Poetry" meetings which were the forerunner to PST-NE

Johnson City:

- Alliance for Continued Learning, East Tennessee State University (ETSU), *Open Hearth* anthology, Johnson City, especially **Helen Hunt Mills** and **Darla Dye**
- Appalachian Christian Village *Tower Chimes* newsletter, especially

Helen Sizemore and **Martha Forbes**

- Johnson City Public Library, *Blue Plum Festival* poetry contest, especially **Daniel Whisenhunt**
- Our Saviour Lutheran Church, a *Mother's Tribute* for Mother's Day especially **Carolyn Bailey**
- *Voice Magazine for Women* www.voicemonthyly.com, especially **Janie Jessee** and **Tara Sizemore**
- Writers' Circle at the Johnson City Senior Citizens' Center, especially **Rosemary Shields**
- Write On! at Barnes and Noble, **Sharon Robinson** and **Lydia Wiley**

Kingsport:

- *Common Ground*, Bristol especially editors **Tony and Donna Kilgore** http://www.commongroundherald.com
- Night Writers, Kingsport, especially **Kayleigh Buckner, Jeremy Maddux,** and **Nick Bernard**
- Writers' Ink critique group in Kingsport, especially **Charleigh Holman, Jean Petke**, **Priscilla Arnold**, and **Linda Dingus**

Memphis:

- Poetry Society of Tennessee (PST), especially **Florence Bruce** and **Frances Cowden**, editors for *Tennessee Voices Anthology* http://tpstn.org /
  Oak Ridge: - Tennessee Mountain Writers, Oak Ridge http://tn-writers.org/

IN VIRGINIA

Abingdon:

- Appalachian Authors Guild, especially **Sylvia Nichels** and **Mary Ann Artrip** http://www.appalachianauthors.com/
- Appalachian Poets and Writers, Abingdon, especially **David Winship** and **Warren Harris**
- *The Howl*, Virginia Highlands Community College, http://www.vhcc.edu/

Blacksburg:

- Virginia Tech, especially **T. Byron Kelly**

Richlands:

- Appalachian Heritage Writers Symposium, Southwest Virginia Community College www.sw.edu

Richmond

- Poetry Society of Virginia (PSV), www.poetrysocietyofvirginia.org

IN CALIFORNIA

Monterey:

- *White Buffalo* Native American Poet Laureate contest, especially editors **Barbara Callahan Quin** and **Wanda Sue Parrott** http://www.great-spiritpublishing.yolasite.com/white-buffalo.php

VARIOUS LOCATIONS:

- National Federation of State Poetry Societies especially former President **Russell Strauss www.nfsps.org**

E-ZINE AND ELECTRONIC

- *All Things Girl http://allthingsgirl.net*
- *Fan Story.com www.fanstory.com*

CONCORDANCE OF POETRY THEMES

(Poem titles A-M in Volume I and titles N-Z in Volume II)

Age/Aging (also see Caregiving, Growing Up, Teen/Teenage, Retirement)**: C**anning Time; **P**roblem with the USA; **R**ed-Hatter Anniversary; **R**emaining, **S**mithsonian Tour; **T**eetering on Homicide; **T**ime Passes; **U**niverse Shift; **W**ho are We?

Angels: Angular Vision; **G**o Away, Angels; **H**eaven on Earth; **H**eavenly Garden of Eden; **S**now Angels; **W**ind and Snow

Anger: Baggage; **C**ommunicate; **F**rustration; **H**orns, **T**eetering on Homicide; **T**emper Temper, **U**nder Construction;

Animal (also see Birds, Food, Insects, Nature, Pets, Reptiles) **B**eaver Retreat; **C**ottontail Challenge; **C**ouldn't a Snake Giggle?;**C**rimson Smudge; **I** Think I Look Like Lunch Today; **I**n Mourning; **P**apaw's Possum Recipe; **P**rairie Dog Native; **P**reacher Said; **T**ennessee Adoption; **Y**ellowstone Park Bison

Anniversary (see Marriage)

Appalachian (also see Hills/Hilly; Regional; and Tennessee)**: C**loudy; **M**agnolia Blossom; **P**apaw's Possum Recipe; **P**ulling Teeth; **S**outhern Lady; **W**hat I'm About;

Autumn (see Fall)

Ball (see Recreation)

Barns: Barn Charm; **B**arn on a Hill; **C**lassy Scarecrows; **G**randfather Barn; **H**ere and Gone, **M**acho Farm, **M**cBarn, **N**ew Way Vane; **R**ustic Barn; **T**obacco Barn; **W**eeping Tree; **W**ild and Free;

Bird/Birdfeeder**: B**lack Crow; **C**icada Blues; **D**ay into Night; **E**agle; **E**arly Bird Routine; **H**awk's Trap; **H**ummingbird Feeder; **H**unger Appeased; **K**ing of the Moment; **M**orning Scramble; **P**ark Politics; **Q**uiet, Please; **R**ainspout Drips on Lawn; **S**leepyMockingbird; **S**now Birds; **S**ummer Hangs her Heavy Head;**T**hree Tanka (Mockingbird);

Birth: Beginning to End; **C**aribbean Heartbreak II (Determination); **C**hildbirth Waits; **C**onception; **J**et Propelled DNA; **L**ife not your Own; **M**agnolia Blossom; **W**omb;

Birthday: Dorothy; **E**rik's Elegy; **E**velyn;

Break Up: (also see Divorce, Loss): **B**lue; **E**mbraced Love Released; **F**rustrated Sky; **H**ole in my Heart; **H**ungry Outside; **K**eepsake; **L**ove's Triangle; **O**bedience Trained; **O**pponents; **R**omantic Interlude; **S**hadow, my Black Cat; **T**rouble; **T**wo Drifting Boats; **W**arning Signs;

Brother (also see Family)**: B**rat's Rant; **G**ift of the Eagle's Feather; **L**ove Spans a Solid Bridge; **M**other's Good-Bye; **T**hrough the Needle's Eye; **U**niverse Shift; **V**isitor; **W**omb;

Canada: Cruising;

Cancer: Annual Mammogram; Dorothy; Hatful; Humans Get Cancer; Pruning Rose; Something New Enters; Thin Promise;

Caregiving: Caged; Clean Break from Assisted Living; Death by Love; Dorothy; Evelyn; Happy Now?; Homecoming; Our Cages; Personal Attention; Visitor; When Mother was Done;

Change/Changes: Altering Currents; Barn Charm; Buoyant Extremity; Grandfather Barn; Here and Gone, Huge Hugs; Lost Again; Natural Home; New Way Vane; New Year Bells; Ode to a Pomegranate; Paddle Around; Painful Love; Patient Love; Places I Once Lived; Rooted; Taking Back;

Child/Childhood/Childish (also see Family, Growing Up, Teen/Teenage): Bumble Bee's Song, Buttercup; Caribbean Heartbreak III.(Child Left Behind); Couldn't a Snake Giggle?; Erik; Erik's Elegy; Erik's Museum Elegy; Eve; Funeral Procession; Leavening; Negativity; Park Planning, Scott's Dots; Spring, March 20, 1979; Waterfall Ballet; Wedding Song For Mother and Son; What For?; Who Gets Him Then?;

Christmas: Away from Home in Iraq; Christmas in Hawaii; Christmas Time Again; Day Before Christmas; I am From; Snow Birds; Xmas;

Clouds/Cloudy: Angora Sunset; Angular Vision; Clouds; Cloudy; God's Paintbrushes; Heaven on Earth; Winter;

Coast/Coastal (also see Regional): Cruising; Luminosity; Sunrise at Cocoa Beach; Taking Back; Tsunami I. and II.; Weather Beater;

Cold (also see Dead/Death/Die or Winter): Gertrude Grace (Olmstead) Rose; Heartless Wind, Hungry Outside; Snow; Snowy Spring;

Communication (also see Electronics/Electrician): Appearances; Beyond Me; Busybody; Communicate; Comparisons; Horns; Hungry Outside; Lonely; Quiet, Spirit Of All; Take War, It's Yours; Temper Temper; To a Rescued Spitz; Word Diet; Words; Worm Spit at Watauga Lake;

Conservation: Contrasts; Day has a Trillion Eyes; Go Around; I am but One; Pest Planning; Silence; To your Health; Water Lilies; World Stage;

Creation/Creator (see God)

Dad (see Father)

Dance: *Ars Poetica*; Black Crow; Caribbean Heartbreak I.; Cinnamon III.; Crazy Poetry; Drip Drop; Free Dance; Halloween Headstone; *Musica, Dei Donum;* Rain Falls; Snow Angels; Three Tanka (Mockingbird's); Waterfall Ballet; Woodland Ballet;

Danger/Dangerous: Detour These Dangers; Dread; Horns; Luminosity; Roaring Twenties; Teetering on Homicide; Temper Temper; Tornado; Trouble; Way Back When;

Dating (see Relationship)

Dead/Death/Die: **A**ll I Want is More Earth Time; **B**eginning to End; **B**erry Diamante; **B**rat's Rant; **B**uoyant Extremity; **C**anning Time; **C**innamon II.; III.; & IV.; **C**lean Break from Assisted Living; **D**ad's Hats; **D**eath by Love; **D**eath - Our Success; **D**orothy; **D**read; **E**rik; **E**rik's Elegy; **E**rik's Museum Elegy; **E**ve; **E**velyn; **E**xpiration Date; **F**amily Cemetery Meeting; **F**at Epitaph; **F**lighty Business; **F**ree Dance; **F**uneral Procession; **G**iant Mistakes; **G**o Away, Angels; **G**raveyard Memorials; **H**alloween Headstone; **H**awk's Trap; **H**appy Now?; **H**omecoming; **H**onoring Mom; **H**uggy Thoughts; **I**n Mourning; **L**ife and Death; **M**omma's Quilts; **M**ortuary; **M**y Office the Day after I Died; **N**o Place; **P**ersonal Attention; **P**oe Toaster Speaks Out; **R**ainbows End; **R**emaining; **R**ight of Way Relinquished; **R**ose Cemetery; **R**ose Petals; **S**uicide; **S**ymbolic Cymbals; **T**hree Tanka (rose petals); **T**hrough the Needle's Eye; **U**niverse Shift; **W**hen Mother was Done; **W**ho was I?; **W**ithout Me in this World;

Diet (also see Food): **D**iet Moan; **F**oiled Again; **P**ear Shape; **T**emptations; **W**ord Diet; **Y**ou Eat Too Fast;

Disappointment: **P**aper Sack;

Divorce (also see Break up): **B**aggage; **B**eginning to End; **G**o on Now; **L**atest Lie; **N**o One Better; **P**acking a Load; **P**ainful Love; **P**aper Promises; **P**opcorn; **R**ose's Other Names; **S**torm; **T**eetering on Homicide; **T**o my Ex;

Doll: **C**hildhood Memory; **C**omfort;

Earth/Earthly (see World)

Easter: **D**ay Before Christmas; **E**aster at Last; **S**o, We Watched Both;

Economy (see Money)

Electronics/Electrician: **A**pril Fool; **D**ead Computer; **D**igitalization; **L**iving on the Economy; **O**de to a Telephone; **O**ld Movies Never Die; **P**laces I Once Lived; **R**ide Metro and Relax; **S**imply Salad; **S**mithsonian Tour; **S**ome People; **W**eather Beater; **W**hat I'm About;

Encouragement: **B**elieve, Hope, Believe; **D**eath By Love; **D**eath – Our Success; **D**reams; **G**od, My Greatest Love; **N**ovember Fall; **O**n On On; **P**acking a Load; **P**addle Around; **P**runing Rose; **R**escue; **W**ipe Your Tears; **Y**ou are Deep in my Heart;

Entertainment (see Recreation)

Fall: **C**ruising; **D**ry Leaves; **F**all Leaf Confetti; **I**ris Gift in Autumn; **N**ovember Fall; **R**epression; **R**ose Petals; **R**ustic Repose; **S**easonal Artist; **T**ime; **T**ribute to Forest Firemen;

Family (also see Brother, Child/Childhood; Father; Grandparents; Growing Up; Mother; Parents; Vacation): **A**ngora Sunset; **B**eginning to End; **C**anning Time; **C**harley Visits Florida; **C**olumbus Street; **D**etour these Dangers; **D**read, Families;

Family Cemetery Meeting; Four Corners; Gertrude Grace (Olmstead) Rose; Halloween Headstone; Huggy Thoughts; I Am From; Just a Sliver of Stolen Crumbs; Late Arrival; Ode to a Telephone; Our Cages; Pom Crazy; Remaining; Rose Cemetery; Seamless Closure at a Flea Market; Slowly Pitched; Soundtrack of my Life; Universe Shift; Without Me in this World;

Father (also see Child, Family, God, Growing Up, Parents)**:** Caribbean Heartbreak II. (Determination); Caribbean Heartbreak III. (Child Left Behind); Dad's Hats; Dad's Razor Strop; Flag Folding; From Father to Grandfather; Macho Farm; Rummage Sale Rummy; Squeet and Twirly;

Feminism: All in a Day's Work; Beginning to End; Daughter of Selu; Death by Identity; Eve; Free Dance; Freedom Fenced; Go Ahead; Lady Like; Life not your Own; Love's Triangle; Ms Muffet; Painful Love; Pruning Rose; Rose's Other Names; Turning Point; Woman - Bitch;

Finances (see Money)

Fish: Truly Peaceful; Worm Spit at Watauga Lake;

Florida (also see Regional)**:** Charley Visits Florida; Snow Birds; Sunrise at Cocoa Beach; Weather Beater;

Flower (also see Garden/Gardener; Plant; Rose)**:** Bumble Bee's Song; Buttercup; Discord; Farewell to Pollen; Flora Sapiens; Flowers; Honeysuckle Moose; Iris Gift in Autumn; Magnolia Blossom; Magnolia Memory; Morning Glory;

Food (also see Diet, Nutrition, Weight)**:** *Avoirdupois* Dining; Diet Moan; Eating Disorder; Embraced Love Released; Fair Enough; Families; Frustration; ; Fun Food Thought; Grits is It's!; Hawk's Trap; Hummingbird Feeder; I Hate Carrots; Icy; I Think I Look Like Lunch Today; Just a Sliver of Stolen Crumbs; Lady Jane; Never Insult Those Cooks; Papaw's Possum Recipe; Popcorn; Red-Hatter Anniversary; Simply Salad; Spring, March 20, 1979; Squeet and Twirly; Temptations; Thermos; Triple Delight Treat; Welcome; What a Pill!; Who are We?; Yellowstone Park Bison; You Eat Too Fast;

Forgiveness: Always and Forever; Baggage; Conception; Latest Lie; Packing a Load; Strong Weaknesses; Three Tanka (My turbulent thoughts)**;** Words;

Friend: Dorothy; Face It; Ford; Friendship; Hooked on Books; Horns; Humans Get Cancer; In Mourning; Matchmaker; Ode to a Telephone; On On On; Reaching Out; Rescue; Risky Business; Roses of Motherhood; Soundtrack of my Life; To my Perfect Friend or Partner; Wild Acres; Words;

Games (see Recreation)

Garden/Gardening/Gardener**:** Beaver Retreat; Classy Scarecrows; Garden of Eden; Gardening Lessons; Garden Path Jog; Harvesting Smiles; Heavenly

Garden of Eden; **N**eighbor's Fence; **S**leeping In; **S**torm; **W**eed; **W**eeding;

Gender Roles (also see Feminism)**:** **C**hristmas Time Again; **P**roblem with the USA; **U**nisex Souls;

God: Adam or Atom; **A**ll I Want is More Earth Time; **A**lways and Forever; **A**ngular Vision; **A**way from Home in Iraq; **B**elieve, Hope, Believe; **B**eyond Me; **C**hurch and God; **C**loudy, **D**eath - Our Success; **E**ach One a Star; **E**rik's Elegy; **E**veryone Knows; **F**lag; **G**od and Country; **G**od, How Much is Enough?; **G**od, My Greatest Love; **G**od's Paintbrushes; **G**reat Creator; **H**ot Air Balloon Ride; **I**nspiration; **L**amb of God; **L**eavening; **L**ife is a Spinning Top; **M**acho Farm; **M**orning Glory; **M**orning Prayer; **M**other's Good-bye; **M**y Faith; **P**atient Love; **P**eaks and Valleys; **P**oet of Life; **P**runing Rose; **S**easonal Artist; **S**eed and Ant; **S**omething New Enters; **S**pirit of All; **S**pring, March 20, 1979; **T**ennessee Adoption; **T**rusting; **W**hat is the Measure of God?; **W**hat's Left?; **Y**ou Surround Me;

Grandparents: Comparisons; **F**rom Father to Grandfather; **G**ertrude Grace (Olmstead) Rose; **G**randpa Swinehart; **P**reacher Said; **R**oses of Motherhood; **S**eamless Closure at a Flea Market; **S**outhern Lady; **T**rusting;

Greece: All I Want is More Earth Time; **C**innamon III.; **E**ver Green; **L**iving on the Economy; **P**laces I Once Lived; **S**mithsonian Tour;

Grow/Growing Up (also see Child, Family, Teenage)**: A**nnual Mammogram; **B**ut, Who am I?; **C**aged; **C**hildhood Memory; **C**olumbus Street; **C**omfort; **D**ad's Razor Strop; **F**airy Wand Star; **F**amilies; **F**inding Mary Again; **F**irst Timers; **F**lag Folding; **G**rowing Up; **I** am From; **J**ust a Sliver of Stolen Crumbs; **K**ite Skeleton; **L**eavening; **L**ove Spans a Solid Bridge; **O**ver Here, Mom; **P**lease - Why?; **R**eaching Out; **R**ight; **R**oots, Leaves, and Thorns; **R**oses of Motherhood; **S**eamless Closure at a Flea Market; **S**oundtrack of my Life; **V**iolin Practice; **W**elcome;

Halloween: Halloween Headstones;

Health (also see Medical/Medicine, Nutrition)**: A**ll I Want is More Earth Time; **A**nnual Mammogram; **B**uttercup; **C**ruising; **E**ating Disorder; **F**arewell to Pollen; **F**inding Mary Again; **F**reely Breathe; **H**arvesting Smiles; **G**o Away, Angels; **G**um on the Metro Post; **M**edicine; **O**de to a Pomegranate; **O**xygen; **S**oul, Body, and Mind; **P**ersonal Attention; **S**pring Greening; **T**o Your Health; **W**elcome; **Y**ou Call that a Sneeze?;

Heaven: Always and Forever; **A**ppearances; **C**ontemplation; **E**aster at Last!; **H**eaven on Earth; **H**eavenly Garden of Eden; **L**amb of God; **R**ainbows End;

Hills (also see Appalachian)**: A**ll I Want is More Earth Time; **B**arn on a Hill; **B**ig Rock Candy Mountain; **B**lue Ridge Horizon; **C**hartreuse Truce; **C**loudy; **C**ontrasts; Cozy at Last; Gift of the Eagle's Feather; Heaven on Earth; I am From; McBarn; Natural Home; *Pahasapa*; Peaks and Valleys; Places I Once Lived; Prairie Dog Native; Seasonal Artist; South Dakota Contrasts; Tennessee Adoption; Through the Needle's Eye; Tourist Season; Way Back When; What is the Measure Of God?; Wild Acres;

Holy Spirit: Altering Currents; God, My Greatest Love; Spirit of All; You Surround Me;

Home: Beaver Retreat; But, Who am I?; Charley Visits Florida; Columbus Street; Cozy at Last; Day into Night; Evelyn; Finding Mary Again; Gertrude Grace (Olmstead) Rose; Golden Ekphrastic; Hammers; Heavenly Garden of Eden; Home; Homecoming; Hungry Outside; Laundry; Living on the Economy; Long Drive; Lost; Natural Home; No Place; Obedience Trained; Peace Chief; Picayune Pests; Places I Once Lived; Quiet, Please; Rooted; Tennessee Adoption; Ups and Downs;

Identity: Beginning to End; But, Who am I?; Conception; Crystal Rose; Death by Identity; Designed Intelligently; Discontent; Drifting; Flowers; Go Ahead; Infamous Unknown; Over Here, Mom; Painful Love; Please Understand; Repression; Roots, Leaves, and Thorns; Rose's Other Names; See a Rose; Signature; Single; Taking Back; Teetering on Homicide; Universe Shift; Vertically Challenged; Violin Practice; Well-Crafted; What I'm About; Who are We?; Who was I?; Wild and Free; Woman – Bitch;

Insects: Bumble Bee's Song; Cicada Blues; Hunger Appeased; Insect Philosophy; Ms Muffet; Pest Planning; Picayune Pests; Please Understand; Rose Dissected; Seed and Ant; Sweet Honey Song; Wild Acres; Worm Spit at Watauga Lake; Worth The Trouble;

Iraq: Away from Home in Iraq; Take War, It's Yours;

Italy/Italian: Ever Green; Foiled Again;

Jesus: Always and Forever; Appearances; Conception; Easter at Last; Erik's Elegy; God, My Greatest Love; Lamb of God; Life is a Spinning Top; Morning Prayer; Spirit of All; Strong Weaknesses; Trusting;

Lake (also see Water): *Grabawil*; Worm Spit at Watauga Lake;

Learn/Learning: Conception; Cross Country Ski Lesson; Crystal Rose; Each One a Star; First Timers; Fun Food Thought; Go On Now; Happy First Anniversary; Hooked on Books; Huge Hugs; Learning Time; Learning Tree; Lost; Lost Again; Mother's Box; My Philosophy of Life; Nine-Year Itch; Packing a Load; Painful Love; Parallel Parking; Please - Why?; Public Forum; Rainbows End; Refocused; Remaining; Right; Roses of Motherhood; Snapshot; Soundtrack of my Life; Two Rivers in One; Understanding; Ups and Downs; Violin Practice; Way Back When; Wedding Song for Mother and Son; Weed;

Welcome; What's Left?;Who was I?; World Stage;

Life: Art Weakling; Beginning to End; Body, Spirit, and Thought; Conception; First I Lived; Jet Propelled DNA; Life and Death; Life is Love; Life is a Spinning Top; Life not your Own; My Philosophy of Life; Natural Home; Paper Sack; Peaks and Valleys; Pieced Together; Poet of Life; Right; Seed and Ant; Something New Enters; Soundtrack of my Life;

Literature (see also Poetry)**:** Hooked on Books;

Longing: All I Want is More Earth Time; Believing in Us; Nine-Year Itch; Pear Shape; Quiet, Please; Rooted; Still Missing You; To My Perfect Friend or Partner;

Loss (see also Break Up, Death and Dying, Divorce)**:** Slowly Pitched;

Love (also see Family, God, Marriage, Romance)**:** God, My Greatest Love; Life is Love; Love is . . .; Love Spans a Solid Bridge; Natural Love; Painful Love; Patient Love; Passion Fruit; Please Understand; Please - Why?; Rain Falls; Reaching Out; Relationship Mistakes; Roller Coaster Love; Roses of Motherhood; Still Missing You; Surprise Gifts; To my Perfect Friend or Partner; Trouble; Truck Driver Blues; Weed; Weeding; What if . . .; What is Love?; What's Left?;

Marriage: *Avoirdupois* Dining; Early Bird Routine; Fifth Anniversary; Garden Path Jog; Happy First Anniversary; Harvesting Smiles; Home; Last Minute; How Much Love?; I Just Need; Natural Love; Rooted; Simply Salad; So, We Watched Both; Sunrise at Cocoa Beach; Symbolic Cymbals; Through the Needle's Eye; Tonight is the Night; Waiting; Warning Signs; Wedding Song for Mother and Son; Winter Walk;

Maryland and DC (also see Regional)**:** Beaver Retreat; Boredom; Cinnamon III.; Dread; Ever Forever; Freedom Fenced; In Mourning; Places I Once Lived; Poe Toaster Speaks Out; Ride Metro and Relax; Saxophones and Jack Hammers; Smithsonian Tour; Snowy Spring; What I'm About;

Massage: Massage Music; Waterfall Ballet;

Medical/Medicine (see Cancer, Death/Dying)**:** Caribbean Heartbreak III. (Child Left Behind); Chartreuse Truce; Death by Love; Erik's Museum Elegy; Humans get Cancer; Medicine; Personal Attention; Pruning Rose; Something New Enters; Thin Promise; What a Pill!;

Midwest: Cinnamon III.; Luminosity; Middle of a Muddle; Places I Once Lived;

Military (also see Patriotic, Veteran, War)**:** Dad's Hats, GI Party,

Money: Christmas Time Again; Deadline Jack; Frustration; God, How Much is Enough?; Gratuity; Infamous Unknown; Latest Lie; Medicine; Pay Off; Personal Attention; Pom Crazy; Recession Obsession; Retiring Labor Relations; Risky Business; Roaring Twenties; Sleeping In; Snow Blanket; Sunday Matinee; Tsunami II.; Two Rivers in One, Ups and Downs; Way Back When; World Stage;

Xmas;

Mother (also see Child, Caregiving, Family, Growing Up, Parents)**: B**oxed In; **C**aribbean Heartbreak II. (Determination); **C**aribbean Heartbreak III. (Child Left Behind); **E**asier; **E**ve; **F**un Food Thought; **G**ertrude Grace (Olmstead)Rose; **G**iant Mistakes; **H**onoring Mom; **M**omma's Quilts; **M**other's Box; **M**other's Good-Bye; **O**ver Here, Mom; **R**eaching Out; **R**oses of Motherhood; **S**queet and Twirly; **V**iolin Practice; **W**aterfall Ballet; **W**edding Song for Mother and Son; **W**hen Mother was Done; **W**ho gets Him Then?; **W**omb;

Mountains (see Hills or Appalachian)

Music: Bumble Bee's Song; **C**onception; **F**amily Cemetery Meeting; **F**lag Constellation; **M**assage Music; **M**ouse Orates Hymn; *Musica, Dei Donum;* **N**ew Year Bells; **P**ast Patriotic; **R**ide Metro and Relax; **R**oaring Twenties; **S**axophones and Jack Hammers; **S**oundtrack of my Life; **S**weet Honey Song; **S**ymbolic Cymbals; **T**hree Tanka (Mockingbird's); **V**iolin Practice; **W**edding Song for Mother and Son; **W**ipe your Tears; **W**oodland Ballet;

Mythical: Collaboration with Calliope; **D**aughter of *Selu*; **D**ay Before Christmas; *Musica, Dei Donum;* **O**de to a Pomegranate; **S**now Birds; **S**pring Frolics;

Native American (see Race Relations)

Nature (Also see Animal, Birds, Clouds, Conservation, Fish, Garden/Gardening, Hills, Appalachian, Insects, Plants, Reptiles, Seasons, Spring, Sun, Weather, Winter)**: C**ozy at Last; **C**ross Country Ski Lesson; **D**iscontent; **E**aster at Last!; **G**olden Ekphrastic; **G**olden Sky; **L**uminosity; **M**y Faith; **N**atural Home; **N**atural Love; **N**eighboring Golf Expectations; *Pahasapa*; **P**ure Raindrops; **R**ustic Repose; **S**now; **S**now Angels; **S**now Birds; **S**now Blanket; **S**nowy Spring; **S**pring Frolics; **S**pring Greening; **S**pring, March 20, 1979; **S**unrise at Cocoa Beach; **T**aking Back; **T**ribute to Forest Firemen; **T**wo Rivers in One; **T**sunami I and II.; **V**irginal Snow; **W**ater Lilies; **W**hat's Left?; **W**ild Acres; **W**ind and Snow;

Neighbor/Neighboring/Neighborhood**: C**olumbus Street; **C**rossing the Street; **E**rik's Museum Elegy; **E**xpiration Date; **F**ences; **F**inding Mary Again; **G**iant Mistakes; **H**ot Air Balloon Ride; **L**iving on the Economy; **L**onely; **M**y Philosophy of Life; **N**eighboring Golf Expectations; **N**eighbor's Fence; **P**apaw's Possum Recipe; **Q**uiet, Please; **R**ummage Sale Rummy; **S**alem, Mass. Hysteria; **S**ignature; **S**outhern Lady; **T**obacco Barn; **W**aterfall Ballet; **W**ild and Free;

New Year: Last Minute; **L**ife is a Spinning Top; **L**iving on the Economy; **N**ew Year Bells;

Nonsense: Around and Around; **D**ay Before Christmas; *Grabawil*; **N**egativity; **S**cott's Dots; **S**illy Smiley Face; **S**oldier; **S**weet Honey Song; **W**orm Spit at Watauga Lake;

Nutrition (see Health)

Ocean: Charley Visits Florida; Cruising; Sunrise at Cocoa Beach; Two Drifting Boats;

Opinion: Editorials; Under Construction; Who are We?;

Parents (also see Family, Father, Mother)**:** Big Rock Candy Mountain; First Timers; Keeping Track of Time;

Patriotism: Flag; Flag Constellation; Flag Folding; Freedom Fenced; God and Country; Hello, Patriotism, Where have you Been?; Old Glory; Past Patriotic; Patriot; Salute and Honor; Tattered Flag;

Peace: God and Country; New Year Bells; Peace Chief; Truly Peaceful; War is Dirty; What Good is War?; So, Why do we Have War?;

People (also see Feminism, Neighbor, Work)**:** Busybody; Captain, Retired; Deadline Jack; Flighty Business; Funeral Procession; Giant Mistakes; Heroes and Heroines; Magnolia Blossom; Opponents; Peace Chief; Pulling Teeth; Salem, Mass. Hysteria; Some People; Tribute to Forest Firemen; What A Pill!;

Pets: Chianti; Cinnamon I., II., III., and IV.; Crossing the Street; Dorothy; I Just Need; Neighbor's Fence; No Place; Obedience Trained; Pangram and a Twist; Pom Crazy; Puppy Yawn; Shadow, My Black Cat; So, We Watched Both; To a Rescued Spitz; Truly Peaceful;

Philosophy: Body, Spirit, and Thought; Boxes; Crystal Rose; Death – Our Success; Designed Intelligently; Drifting; Go Away, Angels; I am but One; Infamous Unknown; Insect Philosophy; Life and Death; Living Lights; My Philosophy of Life; Snapshot;

Plants (also see Flowers, Garden/Gardening, Rose)**:** Chartreuse Truce; Drought; Drought's Rain; Dry Leaves; Ears of Corn; Ever Forever; Fall Leaf Confetti; Go Around; Grassroots; Honeysuckle Moose; Hope Revealed; November Fall; Palmetto; Roots, Leaves, and Thorns; Seasonal Artist; Snowy Spring; Summer Hangs Her Heavy Head; Truly Peaceful; Water Lilies; Weed; Weeding; Weeping Tree; Wild and Free; Woodland Ballet;

Poet/Poetry**:** *Ars Poetica;* April Fool; Art Weakling; Billy Collins; Collaboration with Calliope; Crazy Poetry; From Whence a Poem Comes; Great Creator; Infamous Unknown; Inspired Magically; Interwoven Arts; Inspiration; Our Division; Pieced Together; Poe Toaster Speaks Out; Poet of Life; Poetic License; Poetry; Public Forum; Ride Metro and Relax, Risky Business; Suicide; Triverse; Well-Crafted;

Poetry Forms: *Acrostic:* Flag; Magnolia Blossom; *Pahasapa*; Patience II.; Patriot; Poetry; Rustic Repose; Single; *Adagem:* Heartless Wind; *Beech:* Our Division; Overslept; *Cinquain:* Beginning to End; Temptations; *Con-*

crete or Picture: I Hate Carrots; Learning Tree; November Fall; Slow Down; *Diamante:* Berry Diamante; Keepsake; Paper Promises; *Dorsimbra:* Foiled Again; Latest Lie; Symbolic Cymbals; *Ekphrastic:* Mouse Orates Hymn; Water Lilies; Snapshot; *Epigram:* Childbirth Waits; Running on Empty; *Etheree:* Well-Crafted; *Ghazal:* Embraced Love Released; *Glosa:* Day into Night; Passion Fruit; *Haiku:* Black Crow; Cinnamon IV.; Dry Leaves; Hummingbird Feeder; Hunger Appeased; Pear Shape; Quilt; Rain Falls; Rose Petals; Sleepy Mockingbird; Tornado, Tsunami I.; Wind and Snow; Xmas; *Heroic Couplet:* Snow Angels; *Jaleen:* Worth the Trouble; *Korean Sijo:* Grassroots; *La'Tuin:* Infamous Unknown; *Limerick:* Neighboring Golf Expectations; Scott's Dots; Soldier; *Litany:* Around and Around; *Lyric:* Peaks and Valleys; *Minute:* Jet-Propelled DNA; Time; *Ode:* Ode to a Pomegranate; Ode to a Telephone; *Pangram:* Pangram and a Twist; *Pantoum:* I am but One; *Pirouette:* Morning Scramble; Neighbor's Fence; Warning Signs; *Quintaine:* Quiet; *Quinzaine:* Hammers; *Reflection:* Indian Appellations; *SCOT:* Refocused; *Senyru:* Buttercup; Deadline Jack; Editorials; Lady Jane; Leering Date; Patience I.; *Song Lyrics:* Sweet Honey Song; You Eat Too Fast; *Syllabic:* Storm; *Tanka:* Angular Vision; Clouds; Waiting; Winter; *Triolet:* Temper Temper; *Triverse:* Triverse; *Villanelle:* Crazy Poetry; Roaring Twenties; Saxophones and Jack Hammers;

Politics: Chartreuse Truce; Funeral Procession; Goofing Off, Park Politics; Peace Chief; Problem with the USA; Recession Obsession; Salem, Mass. Hysteria; So, Why do we have War?; Take War, it's Yours; Worm Spit at Watauga Lake;

Pray/Prayer: Believe, Hope, Believe; Beyond Me; Charley Visits Florida; Childbirth Waits; Erik's Elegy; Inspiration; Morning Prayer; Mother's Good-bye; Seed and Ant; Soul, Body, and Mind;

Quilt: Charley Visits Florida; Complicated or Plain; Dorothy; Evelyn; Gertrude Grace (Olmstead) Rose; Momma's Quilts; Mother's Box; Quilt; Quilting Creation; Squeet and Twirly; Stitch by Stitch;

Race Relations: Daughter of *Selu*; Ears of Corn; Flora Sapiens; Gift of the Eagle's Feather; Huge Hugs; Indian Appellations; Old Glory; *Pahasapa;* Peace Chief; Problem with the USA; What is the Measure of God?; Who are We?;

Recovery (see Survive/Survival)

Recreation: Cross Country Ski Lesson; Fair Enough; Flea Market Possession; Goofing Off; Hot Air Balloon Ride; Neighboring Golf Expectations; Old Movies Never Die; Our Division; Park Planning; Papaw's Possum Recipe; Rustic Pom Crazy; Pulling Teeth; Red-Hatter Anniversary; Risky Business; Roaring Twenties; Roller Coaster Love; Rummage Sale Rummy; Rustic Repose; Salem,

Mass. Hysteria; **S**eamless Closure at a Flea Market; **S**leeping In; **S**lowly Pitched; **S**mithsonian Tour; **S**now Angels; **S**o, We Watched Both; **S**unday Matinee; **T**hrown Off; **T**urning Point; **T**wo Drifting Boats; **W**ho Was I?; **Y**ellowstone Park Bison;

Regional (also see Appalachian, Coastal, Florida, Greece, Iraq, Maryland and DC, Midwest, South Carolina, South Dakota, Southwest, Tennessee, Wyoming)**:** **M**iddle of a Muddle;

Reincarnation: Beginning to End; **B**ody, Spirit, and Thought; **D**eadline Jack; **D**eath - Our Success; **D**esigned Intelligently, **D**rifting, **P**ieced Together; **R**eincarnation; **T**o my Perfect Friend or Partner;

Relationship (See also Break-up; Divorce; Loss, Romance, or Virgin)**: A**ll in a Day's Work; **B**elieving in Us; **B**erry Diamante; **B**lue Eyes; **C**aribbean Heartbreak I.; **C**aribbean Heartbreak II. (Determination); **C**ommunicate; **C**ompliments; **C**ontemplation; **Relationship** (cont.) **D**etour these Dangers; **D**iscontent; **D**iscord; **E**ver Green; **F**ences; **F**lighty Business; **F**rustration; **G**ravitational Pull; **H**ole in my Heart; **K**eepsake; **L**eering Date; **L**ove is . . .; **M**agnolia Memory; **M**atchmaker; **O**verslept; **P**aper Sack; **P**uttin' on Weight; **Q**uiet; **R**eaching Out; **R**elationship Mistakes; **R**epression; **R**oller Coaster Love; **R**omantic Interlude; **S**hadow, my Black Cat; **S**ilence; **S**ingle; **S**till Missing You; **T**emper Temper; **T**o my Perfect Friend or Partner; **T**rouble; **T**ruck Driver Blues; **T**wo Drifting Boats; **U**nderstanding; **V**irginity Unlocked; **W**hat if . . .; **W**hat I'm About; **W**hat is Love?;

Reptiles: Couldn't a Snake Giggle?; **G**ertrude Grace (Olmstead) Rose; **W**ater Lilies;

Religion (see also Angels, Christmas, Easter, God, Heaven, Holy Spirit, Jesus, Spirit)**: C**hartreuse Truce; **C**hurch and God; **G**arden of Eden; **L**eavening; **L**ife is a Spinning Top; **M**y Faith; **P**atriot; **P**reacher Said;

Retirement: Captain, Retired; **G**od, How Much is Enough?; **K**eeping Track of Time; **L**ate Arrival; **N**o Place; **P**laces I Once Lived; **R**etiring Labor Relations; **S**leeping In; **S**lowly Pitched; **S**queet and Twirly; **T**ennessee Adoption; **W**ithout Me in this World;

Rose (also see Flower)**: O**pen the Rosebud; **P**oe Toaster Speaks Out; **P**runing Rose; **R**ooted; **R**ose Cemetery; **R**ose Dissected; **R**ose Petals; **R**ose's Other Names; **R**oses of Motherhood; **S**ee a Rose; **S**torm; **T**hree Tanka (Rose petals); **U**niverse Shift; **W**hat I'm About; **W**ho was I?; **W**orth the Trouble;

Science (also see Stars) **A**dam or Atom; **J**et Propelled DNA;

Seasons/Seasonal (also see Fall, Spring, Summer, Winter)**: K**ite Skeleton; **L**iving on the Economy; **S**ummer Diamante; **T**ime; **R**ainspout Drips on Lawn;

Seasonal Artist; Tourist Season; Under Construction;

Shop/Shopping (see Money)

Sing/Song (see Music)

Sky (also see Cloud, Moon, Rainbow, Sun)**:** Frustrated Sky; Golden Sky; Sunrise at Cocoa Beach; Winter;

Snow/Snowy**:** (see Nature or Winter)

Soldier (also see Veteran or War)**:** Away from Home in Iraq; Salute and Honor; Soldier; War is Dirty;

Soul (also see Holy Spirit, Reincarnation, Spirit/Spiritual)**:** Altering Currents; Body, Spirit, and Thought; Boxed In; Boxes; Conception; Death - Our Success; Designed Intelligently; Drifting; Embraced Love Released; Flea Market Possession; Go Ahead; God, my Greatest Love; Halloween Headstone; Mother's Box; *Musica, Dei Donum;* My Faith; Open the Rosebud; Peaks and Valleys; Rainbows End; Refocused; Snow Angels; Soul, Body, and Mind; Suicide; Through the Needle's Eye; To my Perfect Friend or Partner; Trusting; Unisex Souls; What is the Measure of God?; Who are We?; Womb;

South Carolina (also see Regional)**:** Garden Path Jog; Palmetto; Southern Lady; Weather Beater;

South Dakota: Columbus Street; Drought; Drought's Rain; Family Cemetery Meeting; Gertrude Grace (Olmstead) Rose; Heartless Wind; Heaven on Earth; Huge Hugs; I am From; Lady Jane; Long Drive; *Pahasapa*; Places I Once Lived; Prairie Dog Native; Rose Cemetery; Seamless Closure at a Flea Market; Snowy Spring; South Dakota Contrasts; Southern Lady; Through the Needle's Eye; Tourist Season; Turning Point; Van Pool; Way Back When;

Southwest (also see Regional)**:** Big Rock Candy Mountain; Four Corners; Snow Birds;

Spirit/Spiritual (also see Holy Spirit, Soul)**:** Crystal Rose, Pieced Together, Romantic Interlude; Soul, Body, and Mind; Spirit of All; Tennessee Adoption; Through the Needle's Eye; Who was I?;

Sport: (see Recreation)

Spring (also see Weather)**:** Cozy at Last; Easter at Last!;Family Cemetery Meeting; Farewell to Pollen; Gardening Lessons; Hope Revealed; Progressively Worse; Snow Birds; Snowy Spring; Spring Frolics; Spring Greening; Spring, March 20, 1979; Three Tanka (Mockingbird's); Time; Weeping Tree; You Call that a Sneeze?; **Stars:** Each One a Star; Fairy Wand Star; Gravitational Pull; Luminosity; What is the Measure of God?;

Summer: Drought; Drought's Rain; Gardening Lessons; Summer Diamante; Summer Hangs her Heavy Head;

Sun/Sunlight, Sunrise/Sunset, Sunshine**:** Angora Sunset; Angular Vision; Ears of Corn; Golden Ekphrastic; Magnolia Memory; Morning Scramble; Roses of Motherhood; Sunrise at Cocoa Beach; Through the Needle's Eye;

Sunday: Dad's Hats; I am From; Snow Angels; Sunday Matinee;

Survive/Survival**:** All I Want is More Earth Time; Baggage; Charley Visits Florida; Crazy Eddie, One Unfortunate Veteran; Death by Identity; Ears of Corn; Embraced Love Released; Ever Green; Gertrude Grace (Olmstead) Rose; Late Arrival; Packing a Load; Pruning Rose; Remaining; Repression; Rescue; Roses of Motherhood; Something New Enters; Surprise Gifts; Three Tanka (my turbulent thoughts); Truly Peaceful; Turning Point; Wipe your Tears;

Talk (see Communication)

Teen/Teenage (also see Child/Children): Our Cages; Salem, Mass. Hysteria; Trusting; Way Back When;

Temper (see Anger)

Temptation: Devil in the Rain, Embraced Love Released; On On On, Temptations; Triple Delight Treat;

Tennessee (also see Regional): Barn Charm; Barn on a Hill; Blue Ridge Horizon; Classy Scarecrows; Flag Constellation; Grandfather Barn; Grits is it's!; Here and Gone; Late Arrival; Macho Farm; McBarn; New Way Vane; Papaw's Possum Recipe; Rustic Barn; Southern Lady; Tennessee Adoption; Tobacco Barn; Weeping Tree; Wild and Free; Without me in this World;

Thanksgiving: I am From; Thanksgiving, Nov 1974;

Time (also see Age/Aging, Wait/Waiting): All I Want is More Earth Time; Angora Sunset; April Fool; Beginning to End; Brat's Rant; Christmas Time Again; Deadline Jack; Ever Forever; Expiration Date; Fifth Anniversary; From Father to Grandfather; GI Party; God, How Much is Enough?; Happy First Anniversary; Happy Now?; Keeping Track of Time; Last Minute; Learning Time; Life and Death; Morning Scramble; My Faith; My Philosophy of Life; New Year Bells; Nine-Year Itch; November Fall; Now; Patience I. and II.; Patient Love; Pieced Together; Retiring Labor Relations; Right; Roses of Motherhood; Sleeping In; Slow Down; Smithsonian Tour; Stop Watch; Taking Back; Time; Time Passes; To my Perfect Friend or Partner; Waiting; Wake Up; Way Back When; What is the Measure of God?; World Stage; ZZZ;

Transportation: Bicycle; Crimson Smudge; Each One a Star; Fall Leaf Confetti; Flighty Business; Ford; Gift of the Eagle's Feather; Gum on the Metro Posts; Horns; Long Drive; Overslept; Parallel Parking; Ride Metro and Relax; Right of Way Relinquished; Running on Empty; Snow; Train and Retrain; Train Thoughts; Truck Driver Blues; Under Construction; Van Pool; Way Back When;

Wild and Free; Yellowstone Park Bison;

Trust: Art Weakling; **B**lue; **H**atful; **L**atest Lie; **L**ove Spans a Solid Bridge; **P**lease Understand; **P**uttin' on Weight; **T**o My Ex; **T**ruly Peaceful; **T**rusting; **V**irginity Unlocked; **W**arning Signs;

Vacation: Big Rock Candy Mountain; **C**hristmas in Hawaii; **C**ontrasts; **C**ruising; **F**our Corners; **H**ot Air Balloon Ride; **S**unrise at Cocoa Beach; **T**ourist Season; **W**ild Acres;

Veteran (also see War)**: C**razy Eddie, One Unfortunate Veteran; **D**ad's Hats; **F**lag Folding; **H**ello, Patriotism, Where Have You Been? **P**ast Patriotic; **R**eluctant Service;

Virgin/Virginity**: C**aribbean Heartbreak I.; **D**aughter of *Selu*; **D**evil in the Rain; **R**elationship Mistakes; **S**nowless Globe; **V**irginal Snow; **V**irginity Unlocked;

Wait/Waiting (also see Time)**: A**nnual Mammogram; **C**hildbirth Waits; **D**read; Ears of Corn; **E**velyn; **G**od's Paintbrushes; **H**atful; **H**omecoming; **L**aundry; Living Lights; **M**cBarn, **R**etiring Labor Relations, **R**ide Metro and Relax; **S**unrise at Cocoa Beach; **T**wo Drifting Boats; **W**aiting; **W**oodland Ballet;

War (also see Soldier and Veteran)**: A**way From Home in Iraq; **C**razy Eddie, One Unfortunate Veteran; **F**lag; **F**reedom Fenced; **G**od and Country; *Grabawil*; **L**ate Arrival; **M**other's Good-Bye; **P**eace Chief; **S**o, Why do we have War?; **T**ake War, it's Yours; **T**ruly Peaceful; **W**ar is Dirty; **W**hat Good is War?;

Water/Waterfall (also see Lake, Ocean, Rain)**: B**eaver Retreat; **D**rip Drop; **F**lag Constellation; **F**lighty Business; **L**atest Lie; **L**iving on the Economy; **S**outh Dakota Contrasts; **T**sunami II.; **T**wo Rivers in One; **W**ater Lilies; **W**aterfall Ballet;

Weather (also see Fall, Spring, Summer, Winter)**: A**ltering Currents; **C**harley Visits Florida; **C**louds; **C**loudy; **C**ruising; **D**etour these Dangers; **D**evil in the Rain; **D**rip Drop; **D**rought; **D**rought's Rain; **E**ver Forever; **F**rustrated Sky; **G**ardening Lessons; **G**ertrude Grace (Olmstead) Rose; **G**od's Paintbrushes; **G**olden Ekphrastic; **G**rassroots; **H**eartless Wind; **H**eaven on Earth; **I**nsect Philosophy; **K**ite Skeleton; **L**atest Lie; **L**iving on the Economy; **R**ain Falls; **S**now Birds; **S**pring, March 20, 1979; **S**torm; **T**ornado; **T**sunami I. and II.; **T**wo Rivers in One; **W**eather Beater; **W**ind and Snow;

Weight: Fat Chick; **F**at Epitaph; **P**ear Shape; **P**uttin' on Weight; **V**ertically Challenged;

Window: Discord; **E**arly Bird Routine; **E**ver Green; **H**awk's Trap; **I** am from; **M**y Office the Day after I Died; **R**epression;

Winter: Christmas in Hawaii; **C**innamon I. and IV.; **C**louds; **C**loudy; **G**olden Sky; **P**icayune Pests; **P**rogressively Worse; **S**pring Frolics; **W**inter; **W**inter Walk;

Yellowstone Park Bison;

Work/Work Attitude, Work People, Commute, (also see Retirement, Transportation)**:** All in a Day's Work; April Fool; Art Weakling; Boredom; Dad's Hats; Dead Computer; Disorganization; Elusive Pen; Face It; GI Party; Gratuity; Great Creator; Hammers; Hope Revealed; Infamous Unknown; Inspired Magically; Keeping Track of Time; Late Arrival; Laundry; Matchmaker; Momma's Quilts; My Office the Day after I Died; Places I Once Lived; Recession Obsession; Saxophones and Jack Hammers; Seed and Ant; Smithsonian Tour; Train and Retrain; Train Thoughts; Van Pool; Well-Crafted; Work; Work Again; ZZZ;

World/Earth**:** All I want is More Earth Time; But, Who am I?; Day has a Trillion Eyes; Digitalization; Fairy Wand Star; Flora Sapiens; Great Creator; Heaven on Earth; I am but One; King of the Moment; So, Why do we have Wars?; Without me in this World; World Stage;

Wyoming (also see Regional)**:** All I Want is More Earth Time; Yellowstone Park Bison;

CHRONOLOGICAL LIST OF POEMS

Poems titled from A-M are in Volume I;
N-Z titles are in Volume II

1960s

1962: Love Is...;

1965: Words;

1966: Believe, Hope, Believe; Death - Our Success; Mother's Goodbye; Over Here, Mom;

1967: Day Before Christmas; Reincarnation;

1968: Comfort; Dreams; Mortuary; Understanding; Welcome;

1969: But, Who Am I?; Heaven On Earth;

1970s

1970: Still Missing You; Truck Driver Blues;

1971: Believing in Us; Blue Eyes; From Father to Grandfather; Life Not Your Own; Please Understand;

1972: Contemplation; Friendship; Reaching Out; Who Gets Him Then?;

1973: Parallel Parking; What For?;

1974: Discontent; Silence;

1975: Childhood Memory;

1977: All in a Day's Work; Around and Around; Berry Diamante; Bicycle; Compliments; Contrasts; Crimson Smudge; Diet Moan; Discord; Drought's Rain; Easier; Erik; Expiration Date; Ford; Frustration, Go On Now, Hammers, Heartless Wind, Hope Revealed, Horns; I Hate Carrots; Icy; Interwoven Arts; Keepsake; Kite Skeleton; Ladies; Lady Like; Laundry; Learning Tree; Old Movies Never Die; Paper Promises; Please - Why?; Poetic License; Poetry; Puppy Yawn; Quiet; Right of Way Relinquished; Rustic Repose; Snapshot; Sunday Matinee; Temper Temper; Thermos, Tornado; Triverse; Trouble; Waiting; Wake Up; Winter; Woman – Bitch; Work; Work, Again; ZZZ;

1978: God's Paintbrushes; Learning Time; Scott's Dots;

1979: No One Better; Painful Love; Repression;

1980s

1983: Fat Epitaph;

1984: Yellowstone Park Bison;

1985: Baggage; Complicated or Plain; Eagle; Elusive Pen; Fences; Growing Up; Hungry Outside; Living Lights; Opponents; Packing a Load; *Pahasapa;* Quilt; Quilting Creation; Rescue; Stitch by Stitch; Van Pool; You are Deep In My Heart;

1987: Grandpa Swinehart; Single; Tourist Season; Xmas;

1988: Luminosity; Ms Muffet; Patience I.; Shadow, My Black Cat; Tribute to Firemen;

1989: Christmas In Hawaii; Couldn't a Snake Giggle?; Crazy Eddie, One Unfortunate Veteran; Drought; Hunger Appeased; Roller Coaster Love; Turning Point; What If; Wipe Your Tears;

1990s

1990: Disorganization; Erik's Elegy; GI Party, Pay Off; Recession Obsession; Snow; What is Love?;

1992: Happy First Anniversary; Pom Crazy; Rummage Sale Rummy;

1993: Boredom;

1995: Popcorn; Teetering on Homicide; To My Ex;

1996: Love Spans a Solid Bridge;

1998: Patient Love;

1999: Altering Currents; God, My Greatest Love;

2000-2003

2001: Morning Prayer; Truly Peaceful;

2002: Cinnamon I.; Drip Drop; Flag; Freedom Fenced; God and Country; Heroes and Heroines; Old Glory; Past Patriotic; Patriot; Roots, Leaves, and Thorns; Salute and Honor; Tattered Flag; Word Diet;

2003: Always and Forever; Appearances; Each One A Star; Easter, At Last!; Families; Hello, Patriotism; Life is a Spinning Top; Middle of a Muddle; Rose Dissected; Rose's Other Names; Roses of Motherhood; Silly Smiley Face; Spirit of All; Strong Weaknesses; Trusting; What is the Measure of God?;

2004

2004: Annual Mammogram; Art Weakling; Boxes; Charley Visits Florida; Church and God; Cicada Blues; Comparisons; Crystal Rose; Devil in the Rain; Dorothy; Ever Forever; Face It; Fifth Anniversary; Flora Sapiens; Flowers; Funeral Procession; God,How Much is Enough?; Graveyard Memorials; Gum on the Metro Post; Hole In My Heart; Home, How Much Love; I Just Need; In Mourning; Insect Philosophy; Lonely; Lost; Matchmaker; Mother's Box; Negativity; Obedience Trained; Ode to a Pomegranate; Picayune Pests; Risky Business; Rose Cemetery; Saxophones and Jack Hammers; Seamless Closure at a Flea Market, Seed and Ant, Signature; Simply Salad; Snowy Spring; So, Why do We Have War?; Soldier; Some People; Suicide; Train and Retrain; Train Thoughts; Under Construction; Unisex Souls; Violin Practice; Virginity Unlocked; Weed,; What Good is War?; What's Left?;

2005-2007

2005: Angora Sunset; Beaver Retreat; Black Crow; Bumble Bee's Song; Cinnamon IV.; Collaboration with Calliope; Communicate; Cottontail Challenge; Dry Leaves; Eating Disorder; Everyone Knows; Family Cemetery Meeting; Flea Market Possession; Go Around; Golden Sky; Gratuity; Honeysuckle Moose; Hot Air Balloon Ride; King of the Moment; Lamb of God; Magnolia Memory; My Philosophy of Life; November Fall; On On On; Park Planning; Park Politics; Pear Shape; Retiring Labor Relations; Ride Metro and Relax; See a Rose; Soul, Body, and Mind; South Dakota Contrasts; Spring Greening, Take War, It's Yours; Tsunami I.; Vertically Challenged; Virginal Snow; Waterfall Ballet; Winter Walk; Woodland Ballet;
2007: Morning Glory; Slow Down;

2008

2008: Adam or Atom; *Ars Poetica;* Barn Charm; Barn on a Hill; Billy Collins; Blue Ridge Horizon; Buoyant Extremity; Caribbean Heartbreak I.; Caribbean Heartbreak II. (Determination); Chianti; Classy Scarecrows; Clouds; Cloudy; Conception; Designed Intelligently; First I Lived; Frustrated Sky; Garden of Eden; Garden Path Jog; Gift of the Eagle's Feather; Grandfather Barn; Halloween Headstone; Harvesting Smiles; Here and Gone; Huge Hugs; Iris Gift; Life is Love; Long Drive; Macho Farm; Massage Music; McBarn; Neighbor's Fence; New Way Vane; Open the Rosebud; Pangram and Twist; Patience II.; Papaw's Possum Recipe; Pieced Together; Progressively Worse; Public Forum; Pure Raindrops; Rainbows End; Red-Hatter Anniversary; Romantic Interlude; Rustic Barn; Summer Diamante; Summer Hangs Her Heavy Head; Surprise Gifts; Time Passes; Tonight is the Night; Wedding Song for Mother and Son; Weeping Tree; What I'm About; Wild Acres; Wild and Free; Wind and Snow; Womb;

2009

2009: All I Want is More Earth Time; **A**pril Fool; *Avoirdupois* Dining; **A**way From Home In Iraq; **B**ig Rock Candy Mountain; **B**oxed In; **B**rat's Rant; **C**aged; **C**anning Time; **C**aribbean Heartbreak III.(Child Left Behind); **C**hartreuse Truce; **C**innamon II.; **C**innamon III.; **C**rossing the Street; **D**ay Has a Trillion Eyes; **D**ay Into Night**; D**eath by Identity; **D**igitalization; Early Bird Routine; Ears of Corn; Editorials; **E**mbraced Love Released; **E**velyn; **F**arewell to Pollen; **F**at Chick; **F**irst Timers; **F**lighty Business; **F**oiled Again; **G**ardening Lessons; **G**ertrude Grace (Olmstead) Rose; **G**iant Mistakes; **G**oofing Off; **G**rassroots; **G**rits Is It's!;**H**appy Now; **H**omecoming; **H**onoring Mom; **H**uggy Thoughts; **I**nfamous Unknown; **I** Think I Look Like Lunch Today; **K**eeping Track of Time; **L**ate Arrival; **L**ife and Death; **L**ove's Triangle; **M**agnolia Blossom; **M**omma's Quilts; **M**orning Scramble; **M**ouse Orates Hymn; *Musica Dei Donum*; **M**y Faith; **N**atural Home; **N**eighboring Golf Expectations*;* **N**ever Insult Those Cooks; **N**ow; **O**de to a Telephone; **O**ur Cages; **O**verslept; **P**almetto; **P**aper Sack; **P**eace Chief; **P**eaks and Valleys, **P**ersonal Attention; **P**est Planning; **P**oe Toaster Speaks Out; **P**oet of Life; **P**rairie Dog Native*;* **P**roblem with the USA*;* **P**ulling Teeth, **Q**uiet, Please; **P**lease- Why?; **R**ain Falls; **R**ainspout Drips on Lawn; **R**elationship Mistakes; **R**emaining; **R**oaring Twenties; **S**leeping In; **S**lowly Pitched; **S**mithsonian Tour; **S**now Birds; **S**o, We Watched Both; **S**omething New Enters; **S**outhern Lady; **S**pring Frolics; **S**queet and Twirly; **S**top Watch; **S**torm; **S**weet Honey Song; **S**ymbolic Cymbals; **T**aking Back; **T**emptations; **T**ennessee Adoption; **T**ime; **T**obacco Barn; **T**o Your Health; **T**riple Delight Treat; **T**sunami II.; **T**wo Drifting Boats; **T**wo Rivers in One; **U**niverse Shift; **V**isitor; **W**ar is Dirty; **W**ater Lilies; **W**hat a Pill; **W**hen Mother Was Done; **W**ho Are We?; **W**orld Stage, **W**orm Spit at Watauga Lake; **W**orth the Trouble; **Y**ou Call That A Sneeze;

2010

2010: Blue; Christmas Time Again; Columbus Street; Cross Country Ski Lesson; Cruising; Dad's Hats; Dad's Razor Strop; Dead Computer; Detour These Dangers; Dread; Drifting; Erik's Museum Elegy; Ever Green; Fair Enough; Fairy Wand Star; Fall Leaf Confetti; Flag Constellation; Flag Folding; Four Corners; Free Dance; Freely Breathe; From Whence a Poem Comes; Go Ahead; Go Away, Angels; Golden Ekphrastic; *Grabawi*l; Gravitational Pull; Hatful; Heavenly Garden of Eden, Hooked on Books; Hummingbird Feeder; Indian Appellations, Inspired Magically; Just a Sliver of Stolen Crumbs; Leering Date; Living on the Economy; Medicine; Natural Love; Nine-Year Itch; No Place; Our Division; Oxygen; Preacher Said; Pruning Rose; Puttin' On Weight; Seasonal Artist; Snow Angels; Soundtrack of my Life; Sunrise at Cocoa Beach; To a Rescued Spitz; To My Perfect Friend or Partner; Ups and Downs; Warning Signs; Weather Beater; Well-Crafted;

2011

2011: Beginning to End; Body, Spirit, and Thought; Busybody; Buttercup; Childbirth Waits; Clean Break from Assisted Living; Cozy At Last; Crazy Poetry; Daughter of *Selu*; Deadline Jack; Death By Love; Finding Mary Again; Hawk's Trap; Humans Get Cancer; I Am But One; I Am From; Jet Propelled DNA; Lady Jane; Last Minute; Latest Lie; Lost Again; My Office the Day After I Died; New Year Bells; Rooted; Rose Petals; Running on Empty; Salem, Mass. Hysteria; Sleepy Mockingbird; Snow Blanket; Spring, March 20, 1979; Thin Promise; Three Tanka; Through the Needle's Eye; Way Back When; Weeding; Without Me in this World;

2012

2012: Angular Vision; Beyond Me; Captain, Retired; Eve; Fun Food Thought; Great Creator; Inspiration; Leavening; Paddle Around; Passion Fruit; Places I Once Lived; Refocused; Reluctant Service; Right; Snowless Globe;; Thanksgiving, November 1974; Thrown Off; Who Was I?; You Eat Too Fast; You Surround Me;

About the Author

I am what I learned, from whom, but I am responsible for how I use that knowledge. Rose Klix

Rose Klix's poetry is as varied as her Gemini spirit. Poems are playful and pensive, religious and spiritual, humorous and s t o i c. Rose celebrates nature, but bemoans the loss of barns. She looks at many aspects of human relationships. This collection reflects fifty years of her poetic accomplishments while she explored writing formal poetry, contemporary forms, and free verse.

Rose grew up in the Black Hills of South Dakota. She worked for twenty-plus years as a federal employee, started as a purchasing agent in South Dakota, moved on to contracting officer in Maryland, then as procurement analyst she wrote regulations in Washington, DC.

Her current poetry studio views an Appalachian foothill in Tennessee. She says, "I finally have a window office!"

If you are curious to know more, read about Rose's roots on a similar page in Volume I and visit her website.

Rose's website is http://www.RoseKlix.com

Made in the USA
Columbia, SC
12 July 2018